Dialectic of Enlightenment

Dialectic of Enlightenment

Critical Theory and the Messianic Light

Jacob Klapwijk

Translated from the Dutch
by C. L. Yallop and P. M. Yallop

WIPF & STOCK · Eugene, Oregon

DIALECTIC OF ENLIGHTENMENT
Critical Theory and the Messianic Light

Copyright © 2010 Jacob Klapwijk. All rights reserved. Except for brief quotations in critical publications or reviews, no part of this book may be reproduced in any manner without prior written permission from the publisher. Write: Permissions, Wipf and Stock Publishers, 199 W. 8th Ave., Suite 3, Eugene, OR 97401.

Wipf & Stock
An Imprint of Wipf and Stock Publishers
199 W. 8th Ave., Suite 3
Eugene, OR 97401
www.wipfandstock.com

ISBN 13: 978-1-60899-701-5

Manufactured in the U.S.A.

All scripture quotations, unless otherwise indicated, are taken from the Holy Bible, New International Version®, NIV®. Copyright ©1973, 1978, 1984 by Biblica, Inc.™ Used by permission of Zondervan. All rights reserved worldwide.

Originally published as:
Dialektiek der verlichting: Een verkenning in het neomarxisme van de Frankfurter Schule, inaugural address at the Free University, Amsterdam.
Van Gorcum, Assen/Amsterdam, 1976, 2nd ed. 1977.

Contents

Foreword by Lambert Zuidervaart vii
Preface to the English Edition xi
Abbreviations xiii

1. **WHAT IS THE "DIALECTIC OF ENLIGHTENMENT"? 1**
   The Enchanted World (1)
   Dialectics (2)
   The Aufklärung and Hegel and Marx (3)
   Neo-Marxism in Distress (4)

2. **THE "CRITICAL THEORY" OF HORKHEIMER AND ADORNO 9**
   The Language of Suffering (1)
   Criticism and Reconciliation (2)
   Theory and Practice (3)
   Is Reason Reliable? (4)

3. **MARCUSE AND THE "EROTICIZATION" OF CULTURE 19**
   Freud and Fromm (1)
   Reality, Reason, and Repression: The Primal Horde (2)
   Life-Impulse and Death-Instinct (3)
   The Fatherless Society and Surplus Repression (4)
   Beyond (5)

4. **THE POLITICAL MARCUSE 33**
   The One Dimensional Human (1)
   Freedom and "Project" (2)
   Is Technology Politically Neutral? (3)
   The Vicious Circle (4)

5. **ADORNO AND THE NEGATIVE DIALECTIC 43**
   Humankind Died in Auschwitz (1)
   Thinking and Suffering (2)
   Materialism and Maturity (3)
   The Approaching Catastrophe (4)
   The Hope Principle (5)

6   **Habermas and Technocratic Ideology**   54
    Technology and Science as Ideology (1)
    Work and Interaction (2)
    Marx and the Snags in Capitalism (3)
    Dialectic of Enlightenment? (4)

7   **Criticism and Liberation in Habermas**   65
    Phenomenological Criticism of Knowledge (1)
    Synthesis through Social Labor and Class Struggle (2)
    The Dialectic of Morality (3)
    Theory Equals Therapy (4)
    Emancipatory Interest (5)

8   **Horkheimer and Religious Yearning**   79
    The Immanent Logic of History (1)
    Religion Unveils Finiteness and Injustice (2)
    Between Longing and Fear (3)
    The Critical Theory Compromised (4)

9   **The Myth and the Messianic Light**   86
    A World Turned Harsh (1)
    The Dialectic and its Many Meanings (2)
    Dialectic as Belief and Myth (3)
    The Messianic Light (4)

    Bibliography 99
    Subject/Name Index 105

Foreword

by Lambert Zuidervaart

THE DUTCH EDITION OF Jacob Klapwijk's *Dialectic of Enlightenment* appeared during a turbulent time.[1] Although student protests had subsided somewhat and the Vietnam War had ended, a deep sense of unease pervaded Europe. I moved there not long after Klapwijk's book was published, to work on my Adorno dissertation,[2] arriving in West Berlin on September 3, 1977, two days before the Red Army Faction (RAF) kidnapped German industrialist and former Nazi Hanns-Martin Schleyer. By mid-October Schleyer was dead, as were three imprisoned members of the RAF. This marked the end of "German Autumn" (Deutscher Herbst) and a turning point in radical resistance to the administrative state.

During the next three years in Berlin I witnessed firsthand struggles among the New Left to sort out the legacy of the Frankfurt School, even as students, professors, and state agencies vied for control of German universities. These struggles had counterparts in the Netherlands and elsewhere in Western Europe. Klapwijk's study of the Frankfurt School, whose members the European New Left often accused of elitism and resignation, had immediate social resonance and political relevance. Although his book did not receive much attention in Germany at the time, I found it illuminated deep tensions that not only pervaded critical theory but also expressed themselves in conflicts over the future of a democratic society.

1. The Dutch edition of Klapwijk's book entitled *Dialektiek der verlichting: Een verkenning in het neomarxisme van de Frankfurter Schule* was published in 1976 and 1977.

2. Zuidervaart, *Refractions*. This book appeared in 1981 as a PhD diss. at the Free University, Amsterdam. Portions are incorporated into Zuidervaart, *Adorno's Aesthetic Theory*.

Klapwijk's study appeared during a time of intellectual transition. Theodor W. Adorno and Max Horkheimer had died soon after their *Dialectic of Enlightenment* was republished, Adorno in 1969 and Horkheimer in 1973. Jürgen Habermas, their most prominent successor, spent most of the 1970s away from Frankfurt and outside a university setting, at the Max Planck Institute in Starnberg. Herbert Marcuse, whose passionate critique of late capitalist society made him a celebrated spokesperson for the New Left in North America, died in 1979. So too, Herman Dooyeweerd and Dirk Vollenhoven, the founders of the reformational philosophy that informs Klapwijk's book, died in 1977 and 1978, respectively. The 1970s were a time of intellectual transition as a new generation took up the projects left open by the founding figures in both critical theory and reformational philosophy. Klapwijk's book pointed toward new directions in both schools of thought.

The publication of an English translation three decades later holds more than simply historical interest, however. Klapwijk's *Dialectic of Enlightenment* provides a sympathetic, succinct, and critical introduction to leading figures and ideas of the Frankfurt School. It also demonstrates how reformational thinkers can learn from another school of thought while probing its limitations and lacunae. It provides a model of "transformational philosophy," as Klapwijk would describe it on the fiftieth anniversary of Dooyeweerd and Vollenhoven's founding what is now called the Association for Reformational Philosophy.[3]

Implicitly Klapwijk structures his book around the dialectical tension or "ground motive" of nature and freedom, which Dooyeweerd considered central to modern Western thought and culture. According to Dooyeweerd, intellectual culture after the Renaissance and Reformation swings back and forth between commitments to our controlling nature through science and technology and to our pursuing human freedom as being exempt from such control.[4] Adorno, Horkheimer, and Marcuse recognize the dead-end into which this dialectic of nature and freedom has driven Western culture and society, Klapwijk says, but they cannot discover a satisfactory exit. Although Habermas's diagnosis seems less

---

3. Klapwijk, "Reformational Philosophy," 101–34. See also Klapwijk, "Antithesis, Synthesis," 138–52.

4. Dooyeweerd, *Roots*. For a detailed analysis of how the nature/freedom ground motive gets articulated in modern philosophy, see Dooyeweerd, *New Critique*, vol. 1, 167–495.

grim, he too, at least in the early writings Klapwijk discusses, finds no way out. For all of them, Klapwijk claims, enlightenment reason, which was supposed to promote and secure freedom in society, fails to deliver on its promises and turns into its opposite.

Yet Klapwijk recognizes the legitimacy of the Frankfurters' concern for human suffering, and he sympathizes with their criticisms of economic exploitation, political repression, and technological tunnel vision. Their problem, he says, is that they continue to expect reason to save us. Here, too, Klapwijk remains faithful to Dooyeweerd and Vollenhoven. Both of them rejected what Dooyeweerd called "the pretended autonomy of theoretical thought,"[5] arguing instead that all theoretical endeavors, indeed all rational activities, receive fundamental direction from outside themselves. More precisely, like all other human practices, theory and reason depend on religion—religion not as the organized practices and institutions of specific faith communities but rather as the spiritual direction in which all of life proceeds.

This is why Klapwijk concludes that the Frankfurters' dialectical construction of human history is at bottom an insufficiently clarified "expression of faith." Their critical theory, he says, has not been "sufficiently critical" to perceive that it "depends on an attitude of faith and ultimate commitment." Rather, "theoretical reason becomes a force all on its own, and faith in the dialectic becomes a self-sufficient dogma. And in fact … the dogma begins to show mythical traits." For his own part, Klapwijk chooses instead for what he calls a "personal faith," one that follows "the messianic light." In acknowledging an "exterritorial" basis for human existence, such a faith enables those that follow this light to "remain faithful to the earth," avoiding both presumption and despair "in the midst of bruised and damaged life."

There Klapwijk's introduction to critical theory ends. As I am sure he would acknowledge, however, this is really just a beginning. One would like to know whether his critique remains pertinent to later developments in critical theory, especially after Habermas completed his "communicative turn."[6] One would also like to learn what difference following the messianic light would make for a critique of contemporary society that matches the Frankfurt School's contributions in radicality

---

5. Dooyeweerd, *Twilight*. See also Vollenhoven, *Calvinism*, section 1.
6. The seminal work in this regard is Habermas, *Theory of Communicative Action*.

x *Foreword*

and scope.⁷ But these matters would require a different project, one for which Klapwijk's study prepares the way. His study demonstrates a deep continuity among Adorno, Horkheimer, Marcuse, and the early Habermas, amid their differences. Klapwijk indicates how this continuity is a source of both strengths and weaknesses. The challenge for his readers is to reach their own assessments about the Frankfurt School's provocative and penetrating account of the dialectic of enlightenment.

---

7. Proposals along these lines can be found in Zuidervaart, *Social Philosophy*, which pursues a "critical retrieval" of Adorno's insights in the light of Habermasian criticisms.

Preface to the English Edition

In the course of history, reason has always been experienced as a special gift of heaven to humankind. Reason liberated people from threats and evils, it lightened the heavy yoke of nature, and it gave individuals grip on their own situation. Moreover, in favored times, it elicited moments of political freedom, justice, and personal self-determination. In the modern era the fathers of the Enlightenment even presented reason as the unshakable foundation of freedom in politics and society.

But wasn't this Enlightenment claim an untenable position? Can reason be elevated as the ultimate beacon of hope for the modern world? Did reason not lose its innocence during two world wars and under dictatorial regimes that caused unimaginable violence and suffering? Did it not afterwards, under the flag of technological progress and rational expansion, produce new systems of political control, economic exploitation, and blind repression? These were the questions that Horkheimer and Adorno and the other members of the Frankfurt School confronted us with and that I analyzed in the Dutch version of this book in the 1970s.

In our century things have changed considerably. The cold war has been ended. The world has opened itself to commerce and communication. Old and new economic mega-powers plan their technological and administrative strategies on a world-wide scale. The question arises: Is enlightenment reason rediscovering its pathway to the future in terms of increasing freedom, dignity, and justice for all the inhabitants on earth? Prospects like these are contradicted by the facts. Technological domination, mass manipulation, worldwide poverty, environmental degradation, widespread terrorism, and financial crises testify to the same societal paradox as the Frankfurt theorists analyzed decades ago. A regime is operative that in spite of its rational aims elicits contrary results.

Here is the fate of our time. Reason is idolized as the ultimate compass for the future but it fails to enhance freedom and generates effects that threaten all life on earth. Critical awareness about these self-destructive tendencies is rare. Experts combat the failures of reason with more reason and without recognizing its paralyzing results. What we need at the moment is a new critical vision, the need for a light—the Frankfurt theorists named it "messianic light"—that is shining from outside on a system that has discredited itself.

Thus I welcome the initiative of Wipf and Stock to publish this English edition, making a wider readership acquainted with the challenges of the Frankfurt School and its critical theory. I express my heartfelt thanks to Colin Yallop and Ineke Yallop-Bergsma, who, thirty years ago, translated the original manuscript with great care. At that time unforeseen circumstances hindered its publication. For now, we adapted a few expressions and statements to the present situation, but the main text has not been changed. We also updated several footnotes. A bibliography has been included. Last but not least, Lambert Zuidervaart, an expert on the Frankfurt School and particularly on Adorno, has kindly contributed an instructive foreword which will help readers to gain a better understanding of the author's position.

Jaap Klapwijk
http://jacobklapwijk.nl/

Abbreviations

CR M. Horkheimer. *Critique of Instrumental Reason*. Translated by M.J. O'Connell et al. New York, Seabury, 1974 (a translation of part of KV).

DA M. Horkheimer and T.W. Adorno. *Dialektik der Aufklärung: Philosophische Fragmente*. 2nd ed. Frankfurt: Fischer, 1969.

DE M. Horkheimer and T.W. Adorno. *Dialectic of Enlightenment: Philosophical Fragments*. Translated by E. Jephcott and edited by G. Schmid Noerr. Stanford, CA: Stanford University Press, 2002.

EC H. Marcuse. *Eros & Civilization: A Philosophical Inquiry into Freud*. 2nd ed. Boston: Beacon, 1966.

EI J. Habermas. *Erkenntnis und Interesse*. 2nd ed. Frankfurt: Suhrkamp, 1973. Translated as KHI, except for the "Postscript" (see PKHI).

ER M. Horkheimer. *Eclipse of Reason*. Translated by M.J. O'Connell et al. Oxford: Oxford University Press/New York: Seabury, 1947.

KHI J. Habermas. *Knowledge and Human Interests* Translated by J.J. Shapiro. Boston: Beacon, 1971 (a translation of EI except the "Postscript"). KHI includes, as an appendix (301–17), a translation of TW-5.

KV M. Horkheimer. *Zur Kritik der instrumentellen Vernunft: Aus den Vorträgen und Aufzeichnungen seit Kriegsende*, edited by A. Schmidt. 2nd ed. Frankfurt: Fischer, 1974. Part I (11–74) is a translation into German of ER. Some essays in Part II are available in English as CR.

ND T. W. Adorno. *Negative Dialektik*. 2nd ed. Frankfurt: Suhrkamp, 1970.

Abbreviations

NDcs — T. W. Adorno. *Negative Dialectics*. Translated by E.B. Ashton. New York: Seabury, 1973.

OM — H. Marcuse. *One Dimensional Man: Studies in the Ideology of Advanced Industrial Society*. London: Routledge & Kegan Paul, 1964.

PKHI — J. Habermas. "A Postscript to *Knowledge and Human Interests*." *Philosophy of the Social Sciences* 3 (1973), 157–89. Translated by C. Lenhardt, For German see EI.

SA — M. Horkheimer. *Die Sehnsucht nach dem ganz Anderen: Ein Interview mit Kommentar*, edited by H. Gumnior. Hamburg: Furche, 1970.

TP — J. Habermas. *Theory & Practice*. Translated by J. Viertel, London: Heinemann, 1974. Includes 142–69: "Labour & Interaction: Remarks on Hegel's Jena Philosophy of Mind," a translation of TW-1.

TRS — J. Habermas. *Towards a Rational Society: Student Protest, Science & Politics*. Translated by J.J. Shapiro. Boston: Beacon, 1970. Includes:
- (1) pp. 50–61 "Technical Progress & the Social Life-World," a translation of TW-3.
- (2) pp. 62–80 "The Scientization of Politics & Public Opinion," a translation of TW-4.
- (3) pp. 81–122 "Technology & Science as 'Ideology,'" a translation of TW-2.

TW — J. Habermas. *Technik und Wissenschaft als "Ideologie."* 5th ed. Frankfurt: Suhrkamp, 1971. Contains five essays:
- (1) pp. 9–47 "Arbeit und Interaktion: Bemerkungen zu Hegels Jenenser *Philosophie des Geistes*." For English translation see TP.
- (2) pp. 48–103 "Technik und Wissenschaft als 'Ideologie.'" For translation see TRS-3.
- (3) pp. 104–19 "Technischer Fortschritt und Soziale Lebenswelt." See TRS-1.
- (4) pp. 120–45 "Verwissenschaftlichte Politik und Oeffentliche Meinung." See TRS-2.
- (5) pp. 146–68 "Erkenntnis und Interesse." See KHI appendix.

1

What is the "Dialectic of Enlightenment"?

PROBABLY NO THEME HAS become as characteristic of the theorists of the so-called Frankfurt School as the theme that is indicated by the words "dialectic of enlightenment." A book with just that title—*Dialektik der Aufklärung*—was published by Querido in Amsterdam in 1947. At that time, however, the book was hardly noticed. Later on, it was principally students who realized its significance, and in the 1960s a few pirated editions began to circulate. The book was eventually republished in 1969 at a time when violent disturbances at the Berkeley campus in California and student revolutionary movements in Paris, Amsterdam, and Berlin had brought Neo-Marxism to the forefront of public attention.

The authors of *Dialektik der Aufklärung*, Max Horkheimer and Theodor Adorno, took the opportunity to say in the "Preface to the New Edition" that although their critique of culture and science had been developed in the grim days of Nazi terror, it had lost none of its relevance in the meantime. Fascism, they claimed, could not be viewed as something over and done with, as if it were a chance interlude in world history or a brief moment of madness. Rather it was like a gong that announced to the world that developments beyond human imagination were yet to come. Fascism was a symptom, just as today the chains that bind the Third World and the renewed rise of left and right-wing dictatorships must be seen as symptoms.

All these phenomena were, and still are, symptoms of the harsh modern world that has embarked on a journey towards a global society of power and automated control. Gigantic economic and political power-blocs are moving towards this total technological integration, driven by internal and objective necessity, and they collide with each other, leaving behind them a hideous trail of oppression, dictatorship, and inhuman suffering.[1]

Oppression and suffering appear not only in the Western world but also—as these Neo-Marxists, to their horror, had to recognize—in countries under communist rule (KV 8, CR ix). Fascism was not an interlude. No, it is the freedom regained after the Second World War that has to be seen as an interlude, a period of temporary relief. Since then the march towards a totally controlled world has resumed, even if it is delayed or perhaps just camouflaged by a margin of individual freedom in the West. However that may be, the "dialectic of enlightenment" is working itself out on a global scale, whether we like it or not (DA ix, DE xi–xii).

The Enchanted World (1)

What exactly does "dialectic of enlightenment" mean? As we shall see, the meaning of the words varies within the Frankfurt School. At the basis, however, is the idea of Horkheimer and Adorno, who relate the word *Aufklärung* or "enlightenment" to the primeval fear of primitive man. Humans must originally have trembled to the very roots of their being at the sinister powers of the cosmos that played with puny earthly mortals. Enlightenment means that the lamp of reason is lit and that humans exert their thinking to the utmost and free themselves from the clutches of this enchanted and bewitching world. We may think here, for example, of the once notorious book *De betoverde weereld* (1691) or *The World Bewitched* (1695) written by the Amsterdam Cartesian clergyman Balthasar Bekker, or, more generally, of the way in which the enlightenment thinkers of the eighteenth century self-confidently strove to achieve maturity. Since then, the *Aufklärung* program has been, in Max Weber's famous phrase, the "disenchantment of the world" (DA 9, DE 1).

Humans have always had to cope with fear of the world around them. In the past this fear was, according to the Frankfurt School, absorbed by "mimesis," i.e. by following and imitating macrocosmic processes in one's own life. Mimesis was, as it were, the umbilical cord that linked people to mother nature.[2] People sought to escape nature's

---

1. DA ix, DE xi-xii. See also Horkheimer, *Kritische Theorie*, vol.1, xi, vol.2, viii. For the English translation see *Critical Theory*, vii. (Vol.2, viii, refers to Horkheimer's letter to the Fischer publishing company, which is not included among the translations in *Critical Theory*.)

2. See Rohrmoser, *Elend der kritischen Theorie*, 26.

threat by uniting themselves to nature in mimicry. They tried to repeat the cycle of life and the rhythm of nature in the dull beat of drums and dance, in magic ritual and mythological participation. Humans abandoned themselves to nature. They threw themselves at nature, and under nature's control they were nameless, impersonal, and collective.

But there are two possibilities for humans in confrontation with nature. Nature can master humans or humans can master nature—control or be controlled (DA 38, DE 25). The *Aufklärung*, according to Horkheimer and his followers, represented a choice for the second alternative. It was a choice for the desacralization of nature, the break-up of myth, the coming-of-age of the human species, a stand for individual rights and dignity, autonomous use of reason, distance between the subject and the object, control and calculations, experimental science, mathematics and logic, mechanization of labor, industrial production, and global traffic in goods and raw materials (DA 19, DE 9). From the dim beginnings of civilization, this movement of enlightenment has been quietly under way. But from the eighteenth century—not for nothing called the age of enlightenment—it suddenly revealed its emancipatory and expansionist aspirations in insolent self-assurance. Primitive terror in the face of nature has swung right around into a strategy of rational *thinking* about nature and rational *control* of nature (DA 21, 46, 189, DE 10–11, 31, 148).

Dialectics (2)

Here we turn to what is called the "dialectic" of the *Aufklärung*. Over the centuries the enlightenment has failed to deliver what it promised. It has changed into its opposite. Enlightened reason is in the process of eliminating its ideals of reasonableness, freedom, justice, and dignity. It is in danger of losing its grip on nature. It is on the point of destroying itself (DA 3, DE xvi).

How has all of this come about? The craving for knowledge and control in Western science and technology has proved to be totalitarian. The craving for power did not stop short at human nature. Domination of nature involves domination of human beings, says Horkheimer.[3]

---

3. KV 94, ER 93. Horkheimer originally had a more positive view of traditional science and technology, as can be seen from his 1937 paper "Traditional and Critical Theory," a foundational article in the Frankfurt School's theory of science. Following Marx, he maintained that, whatever our criticism of society, the intellectual technique of control

Humans and society become rationally dominated, and within these power-structures human beings can no longer be human. They lose their individual significance, their unique value. The meaning of being human is now reduced to the function that human beings fulfil within industrialized society.

Who is to be held responsible for this development? Not a single dictator, not some particular class of oppressors. Humans have trapped themselves in the spiral of guilt and tragedy. Humans are both oppressed and oppressor, not only victims but also instruments of oppression, taking their share of guilt and paying their share of tribute in the social system. Humanity is deformed by the social structures but mutilates itself as well. For the greater glory of technical ingenuity all other functions of the human self are discredited (KV 153, ER 162). Humans have degraded themselves into instruments or objects. Worker and industrialist alike have degenerated into extensions of the established order.

In this light it is fair to speak of a dialectic, a reversal in world history. Having emerged from a harsh and pitiless nature, human beings sink back into harsh and inhuman forms of existence. The expansive urge of Westerners to grasp and regulate the entirety of physical and human nature has become the independent principle of blind power (DA 48, DE 33), later succinctly termed the *Prinzip Herrschaft* by Adorno. It is as if blind nature, now working under the fancy name of social order, is once more playing with humans.

The consequences are serious, especially for humans themselves. The *Aufklärung* has made an about-turn into mythology and mimesis. Mythical faith in the cycle of seasons returns as mythical veneration for the laws of nature discovered by science. To control nature, humans must and do adapt themselves to nature and nature's laws. Free thought destroys itself as the instrument of adaptation and repetition (DA 48,

---

over nature ought to be developed as far as possible (Horkheimer, *Critical Theory*, 216). Nevertheless, the theme of the dialectic of enlightenment is already to be found here in principle. The critical social theory can in fact be summarized, he says, in the existential judgment "that the basic form of the historically given commodity economy on which modern history rests contains in itself the internal and external tensions of the modern era; it generates these tensions over and over again in an increasingly heightened form; and after a period of progress, development of human powers, and emancipation for the individual, after an enormous extension of human control over nature, it finally hinders further development and drives humanity into a new barbarism."

18, DE 33, 8). With all of this comes a new mythicization of reality. The language of positive facts has become sacrosanct (DA x, DE xii).

Thus the mimetic impulse, primitive adaptation to lifeless nature—despite the taboo on it—is far from conquered in the modern world.[4] It has seized our economic existence; it has been rationalized in the automated instruction of mental processes. The dull thudding of the factory, the drill of disciplined labor, and the restless routine of hard work and clocking on and off are the heartbeat of modern life. It is a ritual, conditioned identification of countless, nameless, interchangeable workers with the production system.[5]

We could speak here of a fundamental alienation. People are alienated from themselves. They are also alienated from the world around them, a world that is equally misused. People no longer know where they fit in, and they let themselves be handled as tools without a will of their own. Sooner or later they can therefore become mere instruments in the hands of unscrupulous dictators who have managed to get to the control panels of the social system. In retrospect, the *Aufklärung* turns out to be not universal enlightenment but universal blindness (DA 48, DE 33). In this way it plays into the hands of totalitarian movements. Fascism was indeed not exceptional but symptomatic (DA 175–76, DE 134–36).

The Aufklärung and Hegel and Marx (3)

The concept of the dialectic of enlightenment is thematically complex. The first element in it is the spirit of the *Aufklärung*, i.e. the Westerner's axiomatic belief in reason as the foundation of freedom and the source of culture (DA 3, DE xvi), a faith whose formulation goes back to philosophers like Kant. In this thematic structure, the voice of Hegel can also be heard, inasmuch as the uncomplicated eighteenth century belief in progress (in the sense of a linear development towards freedom and light) had to make room for the dialectic principle, i.e. Hegel's idea that it is only through oppositions that historical development can reach glorious freedom. Further, the thematic structure also contains a good dose

---

4. KV 113, ER 115–16. According to Adorno the mimetic taboo especially affects any art which is authentic, "the refuge of mimetic behaviour," *Ästhetische Theorie*, 178, 86.

5. DA 189–90, 27, DE 148–49, 16. An early kindred spirit of Horkheimer, Walter Benjamin, had already pointed to the mythical repetitiveness in capitalism. Benjamin also had a rather speculative notion of the origin of human language. See Benjamin's "Lehre vom Ähnlichen" and Habermas's "Bewußtmachende oder rettende Kritik," 23ff., 189f.

of crisis-philosophy, for faith in progress is abandoned and dialectical reversal is explained as dialectical decline. *Progression* is interpreted as *re*gression. It is on this issue that the Frankfurt scholars can tie in with Schopenhauer's pessimism (Horkheimer), Nietzsche's nihilism (Adorno) or Freud's or Heidegger's critique of culture (Marcuse). Finally, it is above all dialectical materialism that has been assimilated into the composition of the dialectic of enlightenment. Here I am thinking of Marx's analysis of Western capitalism as a system in which humans wanted, by means of labor, to free themselves from nature, but in which they have nevertheless ended up alienated from themselves by their enslavement to the world of so-called "commodities." Economic goods, which are actually the result of human and social work, have been made into something independent and given mythological expression.[6]

In all of this we are dealing with a form of "Neo"-Marxism. All sorts of key points in Marx's teachings have been pushed aside, including the theory of the class struggle and the idea of the proletariat as a revolutionary subject in the making. In the Neo-Marxist view, as we have already mentioned, even the workers are enveloped by the established order. The web of myth has been woven across all strata and classes of the population. Here is to be found the prime reason for the Neo-Marxists' cultural pessimism. It is also why Marx's doctrine of an ideal society has evaporated. Horkheimer hardly mentions it, and then only in terms of a "utopia" (KV 173, ER 186).

Neo-Marxism in Distress (4)

Neo-Marxism is in distress because it mistrusts the Enlightenment but nevertheless cannot see how Western thought can deploy itself outside of the *Aufklärung* tradition. On the one hand, the Frankfurt School theorists want to cling to the idea of self-enlightening reason, and they reject all romantic irrationalism as fruitless escape. On the other hand, they are forced to brand reason as the "instrument of power" that is party to the "fault" of cohesive social blindness (DA 45–48, DE 31–33). And it

---

6. Marx spoke in this connection of the "fetishism of commodities," i.e. the mythical and metaphysical projection of the social character of work on to the products themselves. Modern man has fallen under their spell as if they were a "second Nature." See *Capital*, Part I, chapter I, section 4. According to Marx this spell is broken once man opts for a new form of production, a view which the Neo-Marxists do not simply share (see 2.4 and 7.3).

makes no difference whether this blindness is expressed in the viciousness of a concentration camp or in the soul-destroying organization of a factory or in the insipidness of industrial art and mass culture.[7]

Neo-Marxism's distress is reason's distress. Reason can order and reason can obey. What reason can *not* do is to free itself from the structures of authority and command. Reason cannot extricate itself from the dialectic of its own development. Indeed, at every step it seems to become yet more entangled. Modern mythical-scientific respect for the given facts—facts that humans themselves have molded!—eventually becomes in itself a cast-iron fact that makes humans powerless and ushers in an inevitable and even fatal development. The scientist comprehends and masters the detail, but the entirety retaliates by making itself independent. Science becomes an uncomprehended power-structure that turns the tables on humans and blinds and stuns even the enlightened self-assured scientific scholar. Mythology has absorbed freedom, even freedom of thought. Where humans neglect thinking and reflection, thinking takes its revenge on them in the impersonal structures of mathematics, technology, and organization (DA 47–49, DE 32–34).

Thus a twofold question arises. First, how can *society* free itself from the dialectic of enlightenment? Second, how can *reason* escape from this dialectic? Here is the crux, the doubly heavy cross that the "critical theory" has to carry.

Before I take a closer look at this question myself, I want to trace how the Frankfurt philosophers have searched for a way out. We shall consider, in the following order:

- Horkheimer and Adorno's ideas in their *Dialectic of Enlightenment* and related publications from the 1940s (chapter 2),
- the problems that Marcuse deals with in *Eros and Civilization* (chapter 3) and *One Dimensional Man* (chapter 4),
- the negative tenor of Adorno's chief work *Negative Dialectics* (chapter 5),

---

7. KV 165, ER 176. I take "industrial art" to refer to intervention by industrial techniques of reproduction in the internal structure of art. This point was brought forward by Walter Benjamin. Adorno considered this industrial intervention, different from Benjamin, as a degeneration of art. See Habermas, "Bewußtmachende oder rettende Kritik," 184, 191.

- Habermas's ideas about recent capitalist ideology (chapter 6) and his critique in *Knowledge and Human Interests* (chapter 7),
- and Horkheimer's religious solution dating from about 1970 (chapter 8).
- We conclude with an evaluation and radicalization of the criticisms (chapter 9).

2

The "Critical Theory" of Horkheimer and Adorno

I BEGIN WITH THE ideas that Horkheimer[1] and Adorno[2] held in common in the 1940s. The most striking point is that both thinkers attack the dialectic of the *Aufklärung* but spare the *Aufklärung* itself. Horkheimer and Adorno's axiomatic starting point is in the Enlightenment, in enlightened and enlightening reason. "We have no doubt—and herein lies our *petitio principii*—that freedom in society is inseparable from enlightenment thinking" (DE xvi; "Wir hegen keinen Zweifel—und darin liegt unsere *petitio principii*—daß die Freiheit in der Gesellschaft vom aufklärenden Denken unabtrennbar ist," DA 3). "We are the heirs, for better or worse, of the Enlightenment" (KV 123, ER 127).

This undisguised approval of the *Aufklärung* determines from the outset what sort of solution Horkheimer and Adorno have in mind. Criticism of the Enlightenment in its negative development must, they say, lead to a positive conception of what the Enlightenment ought to be. "The critique of enlightenment . . . is intended to prepare a positive concept of enlightenment which liberates it from its entanglement in blind domination" (DA 6, DE xviii). Confronted by what Horkheimer

1. M. Horkheimer, born in Stuttgart in 1895, became professor of social philosophy at the University of Frankfurt-am-Main in 1930 and in the following year also director of the Institute for Social Research (*Institut für Sozialforschung*) which had been set up in 1923. As a Jew, he left Germany in 1933, and in 1934 found a place for his Institute at Columbia University in New York, where he was joined by his Frankfurt colleagues, including Marcuse and later Adorno. In 1949 he and Adorno returned to Frankfurt. He retired from the Institute in 1958 and died in 1973.

2. T. W. Adorno was born in Frankfurt in 1903 and worked with Horkheimer from 1930. In 1934 he went to Oxford but in 1938 rejoined the Institute for Social Research, which was by then in New York. In 1949 he was appointed professor of philosophy and sociology at the University of Frankfurt and succeeded Horkheimer as director in 1958 of the Institute, which had been re-established there in 1950. He died in 1969.

has called the "eclipse of reason,"[3] the authors look for a way out. The following issues are central in their discussion:

(1) the need to think radically about oneself and about the evidence of language,

(2) the demand for emancipatory criticism and for reconciliation to nature,

(3) the actualization of the Enlightenment in the context of theory and practice.

The Language of Suffering (1)

Reason's radical self-consideration or self-criticism ought really to amount to a total unmasking of the apparent inevitability with which prevailing reason and rationality structures force themselves on us. According to Horkheimer, however, this is an impossible task. To perform it, we would have to place ourselves outside reality and outside the prevailing tradition. The critical philosopher himself is a prisoner of reason's empire and is not capable of such a show-down. What does seem possible is a critique that, while remaining immanent, yet has a transcendental direction, namely, towards its starting point in Western cultural reality. It must be feasible, working from the inside, to pinpoint the intolerable tension in our cultural system, the antagonism of reason and nature (KV 165, ER 177).

Reason and nature have not left each other unscathed. Reason has alienated itself from nature and in doing so has been alienated from itself. Particularly in science, reason is just not reasonable any longer. And that is indeed hard to deny. The rigid logic with which science sets about controlling nature shows how exploited nature has got its own back. In preserving itself over against nature, science is actually carrying on the self-preservation that is peculiar to nature. This is what Horkheimer calls the revenge or revolt of nature. Violated nature avenges itself on humanity. The mind is no more than an element of nature as long as it persists in opposing nature, says Horkheimer (KV 131, ER 136–37).

All in all, the mind needs to give radical consideration to itself and its historical origin. People will have to realize that autonomous thought,

---

3. This was the title of the original version, published in America, of what later became the first part of *Kritik der instrumentellen Vernunft*.

which enabled them to rise up out of nature, has begun to claim them by force. The "mechanism of compulsion" that humans have observed in nature is now showing up and persisting in human thinking (DA 45, DE 31). The human subject has stood apart from nature and made nature an object to be dominated. Radical self-consideration must now be the means of getting at this torturing rupture of subject and object. For it is this rupture or "split" that is responsible for the scars on the body of tamed nature as well as the calluses on the hands of dominating thinking. From these calloused hands radical knowledge can learn to understand its affinity with nature. Human knowledge can come to see itself as torn nature, as something that has been torn away from nature itself (DA 45–46, DE 30–32).

For this radical "self-recognition" of the mind (DE 31; "Selbsterkenntnis des Geistes," DA 46), humans are, according to Horkheimer, dependent on the testimony of art, language, and philosophy. Art, language, and philosophy betray the oppression of nature. They give vent to the repressed mimetic impulse. Especially the universal medium of language leaves a bright trail of longing down through history, a trail of yearning ("Sehnsucht") that wells up out of suppressed nature and enslaved humanity. Language—to the extent that it has not yet ended up in the pulp mills of mass culture or in the propaganda factories of fascism—is a reflex of suffering (KV 167, ER 179). Language and literature reveal what is actually going on in the real world. Their truth is "the correspondence of language to reality" (KV 168, ER 180). The values and ideas of culture, contained in language, are "nature's protestations against her plight," expressions of the mimetic life-impulse, rare testimonies of authentic distress.[4]

Such testimonies come to expression, above all, in the philosophy of the *Aufklärung*. Horkheimer mentions such ideas as human dignity, justice, individuality, freedom, equality, and brotherhood (KV 166, 169, ER 177ff). These ideas were banners of freedom. They were raised and held high as general norms that turned against the concrete social

---

4. KV 169, 112, ER 182, 114–15. In 1930 Horkheimer had already given a sociocritical assessment of the utopian ideas of the Renaissance thinkers Thomas More and Campanella. He characterized their ideas as "the expression of the despairing classes who had to carry the costs of the transition from one form of economy to another" ("der Ausdruck der verzweifelten Schichten, welche die Unkosten des Überganges zwischen zwei Wirtschaftsformen zu tragen hatten"). See section 3, dealing with "the Utopia" of his *Anfänge*.

systems of suppression in which they had first been nourished. Human dignity was once the personal nimbus of privileged potentates, but from the era of the Enlightenment onwards it was elevated into a universal characteristic of a more humane form of society. The same goes for other ideas. Sooner or later, often under great pressure, principles of limited or private application met with a wide response in language and achieved universal import. If we look carefully we can therefore perceive two sides to the history of culture. On the one hand is a "barbarizing tendency," on the other the starry trail of language, symptom of a "humanistic outlook" (KV 173, ER 186).

Criticism and Reconciliation (2)

Yet this second trend must also be looked at suspiciously. For the ideas of freedom, equality, and justice, general cries of distress rising up from oppressed life, are all too easily blown up into absolute truths beyond time and space, into eternal principles. But if this happens, they deny their birthplace in history and block historical development. An emancipatory critique is therefore required.

In other words, philosophy has a double critical function. On the one hand it ought to call attention to the discrepancy between language and reality, to the disparity between the existing barbaric order and the general cultural ideas that have sprung from it. On the other hand philosophy ought to subject these cultural ideas to critical examination and to call attention to their provisional, historically relative value. True philosophy is thus doubly negative. It is negative because it resists the aggressive claims of an existing reality. It is also negative because it takes a stand against the absolute pretensions of a prevailing ideology (KV 170, ER 182). Only in this way, saying "no" on two sides, can reason steer past both. There is no other way that reason can be an emancipator, no other way that the truth can free itself (KV 166, 169, ER 177, 182). And this must keep happening, for negation ought never to come to a halt (DA 204, DE 160–61).

The purpose of such a radical critique, with its own origins and history, will be obvious. Radical self knowledge or "self-recognition" and criticism will have to cut a path leading out of the collisions and conflicts in the culture in order to pacify nature and be reconciled to it. It is an open question whether our age will want to take this path. The unruliness of nature and the social order will continue to be a constant challenge to the technocrats and bureaucrats to keep trying to bend the world to their will. By this they show that they have not understood the present crisis nor learned anything from it. Indeed, for all their good intentions, they can only aggravate the crisis.

We ought to adopt a different attitude to nature, one that Horkheimer describes with the words "modesty" and "humility" (KV 120, ER 124). It is an attitude that pursues the moderation or mitigation of cultural expansion and that is also prepared to forgo power (DA 46-48, DE 31-34). It will be a great change. The human spirit must itself want to be an instrument, must want to become a path leading to reconciliation with nature (KV 165, ER 177). It must learn to see itself once more within the context of nature. "By modestly confessing itself to be power and thus being taken back into nature, mind rids itself of the very claim to mastery which had enslaved it to nature" (DA 46, DE 31). What Horkheimer seems to have in mind is a world in which the unbridled activism of Western technology has been brought to a halt and in which human individuality can expand in alliance with nature. In short, Horkheimer appears to imagine the future earth as "a place of contemplation and delight" ("Ort der Kontemplation und der Freude") without venturing into a more detailed account (KV 152, 145, ER 160-61, 153).

Theory and Practice (3)

At this point it may seem as if Horkheimer and Adorno do in fact want to abandon the path of the enlightenment. It may seem that their vision lapses back into a romanticizing mysticism, an intuitive experiencing of an all-embracing nature. But this is only a surface impression. So far as Horkheimer and Adorno are concerned, nature as we know it is anything but an embracing foundation and refuge. Quite the reverse, nature and spirit are divided off from each other. And this disastrous rift can be known and healed only by critical thought and concrete negation (KV 164, ER 175). The light of reason is urgently needed. It is not romanticism but the *Aufklärung* for which we must opt (DA 48, DE 33).

The position of these Neo-Marxists becomes clearer. Their expectation for the future may well be labeled romantic, but the order of the day is tough criticism of society. Anyone who elevates battered nature to a principle and neglects critical reason will fall back into primitive, barbaric forms of existence and will not help to solve the crisis of society. Reconciliation with nature, according to Horkheimer, is made possible only by unfettering what seems to be the opposite of nature, namely independent thought. We are still heirs of the *Aufklärung* and technical progress (KV 123, ER 127). There is no way back.

For Horkheimer and Adorno, the word *Aufklärung* thus has a double connotation: "Enlightenment is more than enlightenment" (DA 46, DE 31). The *Aufklärung* is enlightenment, but at the same time it sheds light on the bastardization of the enlightenment. Or, to put it another way, as an organ of adaptation and as an instrument of the principle of blind power, the *Aufklärung* is degenerate and destructive. But as radical self-consideration it can still come into its own and it can become mindful of alienated and unreconciled nature *in* its own subjectivity (DA 47–49, DE 32–34). The dialectic of enlightenment can still come good in self-reflection. The enlightenment may yet at the eleventh hour reach its elevation or fulfillment—provided it hears the heartbeat of nature in its own breast, provided it adjusts itself to immediate, concrete, practical aims, provided it turns to the world as its own land of origin (DA 49, DE 33).

Enlightened thinking will therefore have to take the side of oppressed nature, its own flesh and blood. It will have to reflect on the world-wide torture that is inflicted on true humanity. In the present oppression, true humanity is suffering humanity (KV 152, ER 161). It will have to give voice to dumb anguish. Here is for Horkheimer the heart of all authentic spiritual culture, of art, music, and literature. "If nature is given the opportunity to mirror itself in the realm of spirit, it gains a certain tranquillity by contemplating its own reflection" (KV 167, ER 179). Here also is the principal task of philosophy. In a world that has become a lie, the philosopher calls things by their real name. The philosopher makes the truth free.

Nevertheless this liberation of the truth, this open window on reality, does not amount to the liberation of reality itself. This "critical theory," as the Frankfurt scholars call it, is ultimately a materialistic theory. It walks not only along the path of the enlightenment but also in the footsteps of Karl Marx and Friedrich Engels. To have something called "true insight" is not enough to satisfy the critical theory. More humane insights are in themselves no guarantee of a more humane reality, of the reconciliation of spirit and nature. What then? Isn't political activism the only remaining possibility, the revolutionary act to bridge the gap between true insight and a more genuine way of life? Horkheimer's own words, back in 1947, were "I hesitate to say so" (KV 171, ER 184).

This is a hesitation that we find again and again in the Frankfurt School, in Horkheimer, Adorno, and Habermas. Marcuse is in this regard something of an exception, as we shall see later (see 4.4). This political reticence on the part of the Frankfurt critical theorists greatly disappointed and annoyed the radical student movement in the 1960s. Activist students even spoke of the weakness of old age and of betrayal. Quite unfairly, I might add.

True enough, before the war Horkheimer had taken over Marx's theory that a better society could be realized only by revolution. Indeed, revolution was also what he was first hoping for when he had to flee to America with his Frankfurt Institute for Social Research after Hitler's rise to power. Yet as the idea of the dialectic of enlightenment, the reversal from enlightenment into blindness, took shape, so there emerged the fear that revolution in a blinded society might perhaps boil down to an outburst of *blind* rage—everyone throwing punches while all slide down the hill together.[5]

From that time on, Horkheimer and his associates were constantly voicing their concern that the political activism of radical groups could hasten the arrival of dictatorship and that it could destroy the remnants of freedom. Indeed, they felt that activism itself could all too easily fall into the rut of propaganda and verbal violence, and that all of this would do more to stifle the voice of suffering humanity than to strengthen it. Let everyone judge for themselves to what extent such fears have proved to be well-founded.

None of this means that Horkheimer overlooks the implications that the critical theory has for social change. On the contrary, in his celebrated 1937 treatise "Traditional and Critical Theory," he characterizes the critical theory—in good Marxist fashion—as just the sort of theory "which urges a transformation of society as a whole."[6] Thus he believes that the critical theory does have a proper practical point to it. Indeed, as he says elsewhere, practical revolutions depend on intransigent theory

---

5. Horkheimer, *Verwaltete Welt?* 27f.

6. In the *Critical Theory* collection, 219. See also his 1940 article "The Social Function of Philosophy" (*Critical Theory*, 253–72). In this second article (271) he stresses that it is only in an extraordinary era, such as that of the French Revolution, that philosophy can become directly political.

and unrelenting criticism (DA 48, DE 33). The only question is whether the dialectic of enlightenment does not weigh down on all of us so heavily that political activism will itself be guilty of the structural violence that is under criticism. Horkheimer is certainly not out to resign himself to the course of events, but he nevertheless gives the critical theory little practical elbow-room in present circumstances. It can be effective, he says, only as a "corrective of history" (KV 173, ER 186). I must confess that that hardly sounds revolutionary.

Is Reason Reliable? (4)

One cannot simply accuse Horkheimer of a gloomy pessimism. He does not say that the doom of the dialectic is definitive. At the end of his *Kritik der instrumentellen Vernunft* he even makes mention of his "confidence in man" inasmuch as humankind uses critical reason (KV 174, ER 187). Yet this immediately raises the crucial question of how and on what basis reason and revolution can still bring the dialectic of history under control, if this dialectic is as oppressive as Horkheimer suggests. Will modern humanity ever be able to free itself from Francis Bacon's dictum "knowledge is power"? (DA 10, DE 2) Armed with powerful knowledge, won't humans continue to subject and exploit the world until they and the world together plunge into the abyss?

Let us take one more look at Horkheimer and Adorno and their attitude to Marx. Not for nothing are they called "Neo-Marxists." In their ideas we do find much of Marx, albeit interwoven with more recent insights. Particularly the tenor of their overall concept is Marxist. Theory must arise from practice and, as critical theory, must turn against practice. It must attack the evils of injustice, suppression, and suffering that have grown up in practice, however difficult it may be at present to forge political deeds from theoretical criticism. In itself, this interweaving of theory and practice conforms to Marx's critique of political economy. For Marx too held that criticism of bourgeois society was a precondition for its change.

Horkheimer and Adorno's criticism nevertheless goes further than Marx's. Theirs is not just criticism of a particular method of production as the cause of suppression and human affliction, but criticism of a collective way of thinking and acting, of a mentality, of a system of suppression that threatens not only a class but the whole of human society, including exploited nature.

The criticism is also deeper than Marx's. There is a sense in which Marx's criticism more or less avoids the issue of human responsibility, because capitalist and proletarian each play a role allotted to them in the dialectical progress of world history and because history runs its course according to laws of inner necessity. The Frankfurt theorists oppose this doctrine of necessity (DA 47, DE 32). To them this is just another token of reason's ambition to control, this time showing up even in Marx. In their view, the crisis of modern society must be brought into relation with humans themselves, with their ambition and self-preservation, with the primeval fear that they nurse against anything they cannot grasp or control. Here there is even mention of human guilt or fault, even if it is spoken of in the same breath as structural blindness, or "a social context which induces blindness" (DA 48, DE 33).

Neo-Marxist criticism also has a different direction. Marx's criticism was directed against capitalist society as a continuation of oppressive nature; Marx's eye was on the realm of freedom *beyond* nature. By contrast, the concept of the Frankfurt School, or at least of Horkheimer and Adorno, is of *all* creation groaning, of a nature that also awaits liberation. In all its parts, reality is bowed down under the antagonism of subject and object, the antagonism of humans and nature (KV 153, ER 162). Thus freedom can be realized, as we have seen, only in a reconciliation with nature (KV 119, 171, ER 123, 183). If there is a connection with Marx here, then it is with the young Marx whose "Paris manuscripts" speak of a resurrection of nature: "Thus *society* is the complete unity of man with nature—the true resurrection of nature—the accomplished naturalism of man and the accomplished humanism of nature."[7]

Frankfurt criticism is thus aiming in the first place not at a change in forms of production, but at a change in the direction of reason (KV 165, ER 176–77). As things are at the moment, it is all a matter of the proper use of the autonomy of reason (KV 153, ER 163), of the relentlessness of the theory (DA 48, DE 33). As Horkheimer and Adorno put it, the fulfillment of that prospect depends on the concept (DA 46–47, DE 32).

At this point, I believe we have come to the central question of this critical theory, the question of its own basis and potential. If the dialectic of the *Aufklärung* is as fatal as Horkheimer and his colleagues would have us believe, if it is a smothering cloud that has extinguished every trace of critical self-consciousness (DA 10, DE 2), can reason really still

7. Marx, "Economic and Philosophic Manuscripts of 1844," 298.

change its course? Does the critical theory itself have a leg to stand on? If the *Aufklärung* has turned "into an outright deception of the masses" (DE 34; "zum totalen Betrug der Massen," DA 49) and if alienation is spread right across our society, can the criticism itself escape this deceit and alienation? By what right does Horkheimer dare to start from the assumption that the idea of truth is still accessible to the critical theory at this stage of complete alienation (KV 165, ER 177)?

The question we are raising here applies not only at the level of cultural criticism but also at the level of transcendental criticism. In terms of cultural history one could still argue that modern humanity is perhaps not entirely under the spell of myth and deceit; one could argue that the fire of alarm and indignation is perhaps still burning in the odd individual. At the level of transcendental criticism, things are different. Here the Frankfurt thinkers themselves have come to the conclusion that domination and corruption of nature come inevitably with the human mind or spirit.[8] Knowledge is power. It is by means of the mind that people raise themselves above objectified nature and hurls themselves upon it. Thinking that is not "objectifying" is said to be "illusory" (DA 46, DE 31). "In the mastery of nature, without which mind does not exist, enslavement to nature persists" (DE 31; "Naturverfallenheit besteht in der Naturbeherrschung, ohne die Geist nicht existiert," DA 46).

Thus we have to take note of the following transcendental contradiction. Freedom in society is dependent on the enlightenment of the spirit (DA 3, DE xvi) but the spirit itself is dependent on the possibility of objectification and suppression. The dialectic of the *Aufklärung* finally arrives at the antinomy of reason itself. At least, that is where it arrives in the thinking of Horkheimer and Adorno.

---

8. Translators' Note: It is often hard to know whether to translate German *Geist* (Dutch *geest*) as "mind" or "spirit" (as recognized, for instance, by many commentators on Hegel, in whose writings the word is of special importance). The reader is asked to be aware of this problem when encountering the words "mind" or "spirit" in this and other translations.

3

Marcuse and the "Eroticization" of Culture

WE WANT TO TURN now to the views of Herbert Marcuse.[1] He calls our theme the "dialectic of Enlightenment" or "dialectic of civilization" (EC 72, 78). Marcuse does indeed deserve our attention. He has made a serious attempt to penetrate the ambiguity of the Western concept of reason in order to get at the foundations of the dialectic of enlightenment.[2] He has also tried hard to give concrete shape to the idea of a liberated society, however vulnerable his utopia may prove to be. And, to mention only one more point, Marcuse offers a profound theoretical consideration of the preconditions for social revolution.

Freud and Fromm (1)

The first thing that strikes the reader of Marcuse's principal theoretical work, *Eros and Civilization*, is that he draws heavily upon Sigmund Freud. It seems that Marcuse wants in the first instance to explain the crisis of Western reason and society with the help of psychoanalytical categories.

The fact that a social critic from the Frankfurt School turns to Freudian psychoanalysis is less strange than one might at first think. In the first place, both Freud and the Frankfurt thinkers want to understand humanity "materialistically," whether on the basis of biological instincts[3] or of bodily nature. Furthermore there is quite a striking

---

1. H. Marcuse, born in Berlin in 1898, became an *Assistent* under Martin Heidegger in 1928 and worked with the Institute for Social Research first in Frankfurt and then from 1934 to 1940 in New York. After that, he worked for the American State Department, among other jobs. In 1954 he was appointed professor of political science at Brandeis University. In 1965 he moved to the University of California at San Diego. He retired in 1969 and died in 1979.

2. See J. Habermas, TW 94 (TRS 114–15), and also 6.1 below.

3. Translators' Note: The Dutch is *drift*, corresponding to German *Trieb*. English-speaking Freudians have commented on the difficulty of knowing whether to translate

analogy between the Freudian theory of instinctual repression and the Frankfurt theory of social oppression. In both cases a process of suppressing essential human needs is involved. Moreover, both in Freudian and in Frankfurt theory, people are said to be largely unconscious of what is going on in this process. On closer inspection, there is even more than an analogy. Both schools of thought hold that there is a structural relationship between instinctual repression and social oppression. In Freud's view, of course, the repression of primary instincts inside the human organism is caused by a clash with the world outside, a clash with the harsh demands of reality. And on the other side, in the view of the Frankfurt School, oppression is not just a social evil but more and more a psychological manipulation. Thus Marcuse uses the one term "repression" to include both the personal repression of instincts and the social phenomenon of oppression.

Marcuse was actually not the first or only member of the Frankfurt School who tried to link social criticism and psychoanalysis. Around 1930 Horkheimer had taken up the cause of Freud's work and had tried to publicize it and organize support for it. Adorno had also shown signs of interest. Indeed, notable psychoanalysts such as Karl Landauer and Erich Fromm were at that time already associated with the Institute for Social Research, which had been set up in 1923 and which was subsequently directed by Horkheimer.[4]

Fromm played a fairly controversial role in this connection. More than anyone else at the Institute, he originally aimed at reconciling Marx and Freud.[5] Later he dropped Freud in favor of a Neo-Freudian revisionism, the foundations of which were laid by Fromm himself along with other analysts such as Karen Horney and Harry Stock Sullivan.[6]

Freud's original term as "drive" or "instinct." We have preferred instinct, which seems to be the more usual term in English.

4. See Jay, *Dialectical Imagination*, 87f., 27.

5. The Frankfurt School has always felt a sense of kinship with Freud. In 1957 the Institute published a collection of papers entitled *Freud in der Gegenwart*. This volume, consisting of lectures given in honor of the centenary of Freud's birth, included contributions from Horkheimer and Marcuse.

6. Fromm voiced his criticism as early as 1935, in the article "Die gesellschaftliche Bedingtheit der psychoanalytischen Therapie" in the Institute's journal *Zeitschrift für Sozialforschung*. In this article Fromm rejects Freud's view that the analyst must be neutral and tolerant if he wants to be able to help his patient. Behind this view, according to Fromm, lurks the idea of a value-free analysis. This idea is characteristic of the bourgeois liberalism in which he feels Freud is still trapped. (See esp. 371–92.)

This revisionist movement produced more and more criticisms of central themes in Freud's teaching. First of all, the critics pointed to all sorts of old-fashioned, bourgeois elements in Freud's thinking. They pointed out his one-sided concern with the human individual that had to be understood against the background of childhood years and biological development; they accused him of neglecting the way in which humans might be affected by influences from the present and from contemporary society. The critics also turned their attention to Freud's theory of society, a theory that they claimed was static and overlooked society's pattern of growth and the "productive" insights and "interpersonal" experiences that were thereby acquired. And, to mention only one further criticism, they also attacked Freud's cultural pessimism and lack of ethical vision, a pessimism that they considered to be related to Freud's scientism and his later hypothesis about the death instinct, the primal horde, the original murder of the tribal father, and so on.

It is not surprising that Marcuse's *Eros and Civilization* leads to a fierce polemic against this "conservative" Freudian revisionism. The main thrust of the book is to present a completely different picture of Freud, the picture of a "critical" Freud. Marcuse is even more enthusiastic about it than Horkheimer and Adorno (EC 273). For the rest we will have to let the different interpretations of Freud that have been put forward by Fromm and his colleagues on the one hand, and by the "left-wing Freudians" on the other, stand for what they are.[7] In our study we can only show how Marcuse has brought the critical Freud to the fore, in order to indicate what is really going on in the dialectic of enlightenment.

Marcuse is well aware that the theory of psychoanalysis is in the first place a psychology of the human individual and the structure of human instincts, expressed by Freud in concepts such as sublimation, identification, projection, repression, introjection, etc. In Marcuse's eyes, however, Freud's psychology of the individual is more than just that. It is at its very roots a "social psychology," or, even more broadly, a "theory of civilization" (EC 16, 106), because individuals with their neuroses and frustrations have to be understood against the background of the social reality in which they operate, or the history of civilization in which they are caught up. Repression is not simply an individual problem but a universal, cultural, and historical phenomenon that repeats itself and works itself out at the individual level. If you restrict your view of psychoanaly-

---

7. For further details see Jay, *Dialectical Imagination*, chapter 3.

sis and see it as a theory of human individuals and a therapy for their repressions and neuroses, aiming at better adaptation to society (and what else could the therapy aim at?), then psychoanalysis does seem like an uncritical and conformist stunt, a handy trick for established authority. But if you see psychoanalysis in a wider context as a "metapsychological" theory of society, or even as a philosophical ontology (EC 107), dealing with life and death and the relationship with inorganic matter, then the theory's "hidden trend" (EC 20) is revealed and the true, critical Freud becomes visible.

To make this view of Freud plausible, Marcuse deliberately turned to Freud's later work, because it was only there that Freud extrapolated his psychoanalytical teaching about instinct into a social theory that was concerned not only with the particular fates of individuals but with the weal and woe of the whole of human civilization.

Reality, Reason, and Repression: *The Primal Horde (2)*

The first thing to note in the psychoanalytical theory of instincts is Freud's now famous teaching that the instinctual drives and needs of a human being are, from earliest childhood, suppressed and transformed by the demands that a civilized society makes on its citizens—demands that a civilized society *must* make. The human being is originally scarcely more than a collection of animal instincts. This being becomes truly human, a human "ego"[8] only in a dramatic clash with the outside world, through which instincts are curbed and channeled towards subsidiary ends. This means that instinctual human values, i.e. the principles governing the achievement of human goals, are altered, and the so-called pleasure principle (Freud's "Lustprinzip") is replaced by the reality principle (Freud's "Realitätsprinzip"). It is only under the influence of the reality principle that unbridled behavior is checked, sexual desire curtailed, and play and pleasure turn into productive work and the building up of culture.

Under the constraint of this reality principle, so the theory goes, humans are forced to use their heads. Only then do they begin to develop the power of theoretical and practical reason to distinguish the good from the bad, the true from the false, the useful from the harmful (EC

---

8. Translators' Note: In English, "ego" and "id" are now standard, but Freud's German terms were simply "I" and "it" (*Ich* and *Es*). Compare Shapiro's comment (KHI 344).

14, 30). Reason is thus developed as a function of the reality principle in order to put the energy of human instinctual life into meaningful service. What Marcuse stresses here is that the reality principle evokes reason and reason evokes repression. "Exploitative" and "repressive" reason (EC 156, 160), which Horkheimer sees as the painful consequence of the dialectic of civilization, seems for both Freud and Marcuse to be an inevitable starting-point, an ingrained characteristic.

Practically all of the human instinctual apparatus has put itself at the disposal of the reality principle and is organized by it so as to satisfy the norms of authority and the demands of culture and diligence. The exception is the power of imagination. Imagination has split off from the rational consciousness and continues to be determined by the other principle, the principle of desire and libido (EC 140). To the extent that it has not been conventionalized in artistic and literary expression and shunted off on to a cultural siding, imagination lives a secret life of abandon, sinful and perverse, hidden away in the recesses of the id, the subconscious. Imagination is bowed down, as Adorno would have said, under the "mimetic taboo." Imagination is thus a sad reminder of long-lost happiness, but also an unmistakable indication that the libido principle can never be completely conquered.

Freud describes the replacement of the pleasure principle by the reality principle as the great traumatic event in both personal and human history. Marcuse constantly emphasizes the latter. Freud linked the psychology of the human individual to a general theory of human civilization. Parallel to the ontogenetic instinctual development of the human individual is a phylogenetic instinctual change in the human species.

To make this idea easier to understand, Freud presented the hypothesis of a primal human horde in prehistoric times. The way in which the tribal father of the horde eventually monopolized all enjoyment of the women and all the power over them, at the expense of the sons, can be compared with the way in which parents and educators exercise their power and authority over children to this very day. This primal venture ended in patricide and threatened to tear the group apart. It was not until then that the insight emerged that the father was motivated not just by power and lust but also by a new principle, the reality principle, serving the interests of the group as a whole. Resentment turned to guiltiness, and the clan of brothers identified themselves with the father and claimed the father's right to forbid and restrict. Indeed, the brothers went further than the father, and strengthened and institutionalized patriarchal authority in order to prevent a repetition of events.

This then is a chapter of social history that is said to repeat itself in each new generation in the spiral of resentment, guilt, identification, and intensified repression. And the parallel is seen in the micro-history of the individual son who, once separated from his mother's womb, moves through to the Oedipus complex of aggression and guiltiness and finally subjects himself to the authority of father and society as the embodiment of the reality principle. He "introjects" into his own consciousness the norms of authority that have come to him through this experience, and he thereby builds up his superego, his nagging conscience.

For Marcuse, the hypothesis of the primal horde has a value that is not so much historical as "symbolic" (EC 60). Marcuse finds it a sensible explanatory background for undeniable cultural facts. At any rate, Freud's hypothesis explains how cultural progress can go hand in hand with increasing domination. Besides, Freud's construction has, according to Marcuse, a hard material core, namely the connection between repression and scarcity (EC 16). The repressive transformation of instinctual life under the pressure of the reality principle is an inevitable consequence of the permanent struggle for survival and the competition for the means of subsistence. It is this "life's necessity" ("Lebensnot"), the scarcity of means, that has drummed it into the human species ever since primeval times that it cannot just indulge its drives and instincts and that human society is simply not possible under the regime of the libido principle. As Freud himself suggests, society must ultimately be viewed in "economic" terms.[9] Seeing that society does not have sufficient means to keep its members alive without work, it has to restrict the number of members and divert their energies from sexuality to productivity.

In short, Freud believes there is an inner connection between culture and suppression, reason and repression, freedom and unhappiness. This connection is depicted in the story of the primal horde, repeated in the birth trauma of every individual and grounded in the "irreconcilable," even "eternal" conflict between pleasure principle and reality principle.

---

9. See Freud's *General Introduction to Psychoanalysis*, 273, and "Introductory Lectures," 374, 378.

Life-Impulse and Death-Instinct (3)

In a number of fairly late publications, including *Beyond the Pleasure Principle* and *Civilization and its Discontents*, Freud expressed the view that the conflict between pleasure principle and reality principle was not in itself sufficient to explain the surplus of power, terror, war, and destructive violence in civilized society. He now looked beyond the pleasure principle to another principle, to which he gave a name taken from Barbara Low, the "Nirvana principle."[10] In connection with this, he mentions another instinct, alongside or behind the erotic life-instinct, the death-instinct. He claims that the death-instinct wants to take life back to the quiet rest of "nirvana." But at the same time the death-instinct must be held responsible for the excess of tension, grief, and aggression in the culture.

Freud sometimes surmises that *Thanatos*, the death-instinct, is even more original than the life-instinct, and that the latter is no more than a leaping flame that sets culture aglow, yet leads culture along a detour of its own choosing back to the ashes of death.[11] The efforts of instincts to work off the effects of stimulation and their inert attachment to a situation of "lasting gratification" could point to life's general tendency to want to return to the "quiescence of the inorganic world" (EC 234, 25). Perhaps the pleasure principle must be seen in the light of the Nirvana principle, and the life instinct set in the context of the death instinct.

However this may be, Marcuse observes that at the level of culture Freud has placed life-instinct and death-instinct opposite each other as equal partners (EC 28). In culture the erotic life-instinct, transformed into a uniting, creative energy, is continually criss-crossed and outmaneuvered by the death-impulse. Thanatos reveals itself in two directions, outwardly in the aggression expressed by and against the authoritarian father-figure, inwardly in the stern intolerance of the superego, the revenge of conscience.

Here again we find Freud's idea that culture is facing a blank wall. The increased aggression of the death-instinct requires strong resistance. Where is such resistance to come from? The culture should be able to mobilize resistance from the vital, sexually directed life-forces. But, sadly, culture means sublimation and therefore a weakening of sex

---

10. "Beyond the Pleasure Principle," 55–56.
11. Ibid. 33ff.

or desexualization. As a consequence, the balance in the instinctual structure is upset. The erotic drives, now that they have been sublimated, can no longer restrain the destructive forces. The aggression-impulse breaks loose and the death-instinct dominates. Culture heads for self-destruction (EC 83).

It is more or less along these lines that Marcuse has interpreted Freud's work. Let us now try to be more specific about Marcuse's personal standpoint compared with Freud's, particularly compared with Freud's later ideas.

In the first place, I think that Marcuse differs from Freud in that Marcuse's "dialectic of civilization" is determined, at its roots, not by the conflict of Eros and Thanatos, but by the collision of the "pleasure principle" and the "reality principle." It is true that Marcuse accepts the hypothesis of Eros and Thanatos (EC 234). But in what way? He attacks the idea of an original dualism of Eros and Thanatos and the notion that life-instinct and death-instinct have always been equal partners in determining cultural development. And he recoils altogether from Freud's conjecture that pleasure is encompassed by death. In other words, Marcuse will not accept that the death-instinct is superior to the life-instinct, that cultural development is a deceptive "detour" leading from death back to death (EC 25).

In contrast to this monism of death, Marcuse chooses a different, erotic-sexual monism, a monism which explicitly starts from the life-instinct (EC 28). And with this instinct comes its regulative starting point, the libido principle. One might argue that the original libidinous man must surely also be confronted with death, time, and transitoriness. According to Marcuse, however, this painful confrontation is not noticeable unless humanity has been crystallized as a personal ego. "Time has no power over the id, the original domain of the pleasure principle. But the ego, through which alone pleasure becomes real, is in its entirety subject to time" (EC 231). The problem of death, therefore, does not make itself felt until the collision of pleasure principle and reality principle has caused the ego to crystallize.

In my view there is another reason why Marcuse pushes the hypothesis of Eros and Thanatos into the background. In Freud's work, this hypothesis is a naturalistic hypothesis, as can be clearly seen in, for example, *Beyond the Pleasure Principle*.[12] Aggressive behavior and the im-

12. Freud posits the need to follow biological terminology in description, and he

pulse to self-destruction in the culture are explained here and elsewhere as natural causes, i.e. in terms of a biological "regression compulsion" and of the relief of "tensions" that may have been due to geological factors (EC 29, 136). The life of humankind and culture is supposed to seek against its will to return to the "quiescence of the inorganic world" (EC 25), as if somehow compelled by the laws of nature. As for the *Lebensnot* of economic scarcity, that harsh necessity from which the collision of pleasure principle and reality principle arose, Freud also gives a twist to it in the light of the death-instinct, making it a sort of biological deficiency in the human organism (EC 132).

Certainly, Marcuse is also struck by the element of self-destruction in culture itself. "In every revolution, there seems to have been a historical moment when the struggle against domination might have been victorious—but the moment passed" (EC 90). Why does revolution betray itself like this? When you examine Marcuse's answer closely, you find it is not in terms of a biological deficiency or an ontological necessity. On the contrary, Marcuse explains this fatal cultural element in the light of the collision of libido and reality, and he sees it as a psychological "identification" with the father, an identification of the same kind as the primal horde once made.

The Fatherless Society and Surplus Repression (4)

Yet Marcuse does *not simply* hark back to an earlier explanatory formula of Freud's. He emphasizes that the power of the father in the modern culture has been replaced by the omnipotence of the bureaucracy.[13] And this bureaucracy no longer needs to fashion the superego by plodding its way along the detour of personal resentment, anxiety, guiltiness, identification, introjection, and repression. Nowadays it is much easier. The bureaucracy has, by its manipulative power, seen to the "automatization of the superego" (EC 94). By virtue of this, individuals are no longer conscious of that former sense of guilt, and their existential angst or anxiety

---

would ultimately prefer to use physiological or chemical concepts. "The deficiencies in our description would probably vanish if we were already in a position to replace the psychological terms by physiological or chemical ones," ibid., 60.

13. "We seem to be faced with a reality which was envisaged only at the margin of psychoanalysis—the *vaterlose Gesellschaft* (society without fathers)" (Marcuse, "Obsolescence," 53).

has yielded to the dubious happiness of a "general anesthesia." Humans adjust themselves like automatons (EC 32, 103).

Actually, Freud's ideas about the instinctual dynamics of the human individual were not exactly wrong, it is just that cultural history has overtaken them. At present the interactions of ego, superego, and id have congealed into "automatic reactions" (EC 103). This, according to Marcuse, is also why you hardly come across individual human beings in daily life any longer. You discover only types and role-players with their appropriate gestures and grimaces. Like Horkheimer and Adorno, Marcuse finds human subjectivity violated. Humanity has been objectified.

The tenor of Marcuse's criticism of Freud becomes apparent. The dialectic of culture cannot be explained in terms of an inevitable and natural doom that somehow represents the reaching grasp of Death. Equally inadequate is an explanation that appeals to the inner secrets of human instinctual life—such an explanation would certainly not hold good for modern automated individuals. Moreover, Marcuse is not unaware that his "critical" Freud had not only a naturalistic conception of cultural life but also, as is evident in his earlier works, a naturalistic conception of instinctual life. According to Freud, the clash between instincts and the external world was simply in man's "nature," so that the social transformation of these instincts was inevitable and civilization just had to rest on "permanent subjugation" (EC 3).

Marcuse too holds that the dialectic of enlightenment has to be understood against the underlying dynamics of the instincts. But this dynamics must not be "naturalized" but "historicized," i.e. explained in a cultural-historical perspective. In Marcuse's view, Freud does not sufficiently distinguish between the biological and the social-historical vicissitudes of the instincts (EC 35). Yet Marcuse generally likes to give the impression that his revision of Freud is no more than an elaboration.

One wonders here whether Marcuse isn't taking liberties with Freud. Freud's concepts are said to be "unhistorical" but nevertheless have a "historical substance" that justifies a historical "extrapolation" (EC 35). Again, Marcuse suggests he is really doing little more than revealing "the hidden trend in psychoanalysis" (EC 25). In fact he is doing more than that.

However questionable this interpretation of Freud may be, it is at any rate clear that Marcuse himself regards the reality principle not as a biological necessity but as a historical accident (EC 34). And its collision with the libido principle is not an eternal struggle (EC 80) but historically limited (EC 129). Thus the instinctual repression and social oppression that result from this clash of principles are not built into human nature as such but arise from specific historical circumstances as we find them in modern societies (EC 132).

The central argument in Marcuse's historicist interpretation of Freud's psychoanalysis is in fact of Marxist origin. Marx taught that an increase in industrial production decreases the objective necessity for social suppression for increasing production will eventually cause a revolution in power relationships (7.3). Marcuse similarly fastens on to the technological chances of the modern industrial age. Freud had depicted economic scarcity as an inevitable, "natural" source of conflict between man's libidinous longings and society's harsh demands. But in the light of history, in the light, that is, of the technological potential of the modern welfare state, that scarcity—and hence all the repression that results from it—turns out to be only partly necessary. Nowadays at least, that shortage could be almost totally overcome (EC 36).

For this reason Marcuse begins to make further distinctions in Freud's basic concepts. First of all he distinguishes between "repression" in the Freudian sense (i.e. repression as a fundamental stifling of instincts, something that is necessary to ensure the perpetuation of the human species in society) and "surplus repression" (i.e. an excess of suppression that has arisen in the course of history through an accumulation of power, but is not justified by scarcity and, at least at present, could be got rid of).

Marcuse also makes a distinction with respect to the so-called "reality principle." He agrees with Freud that individuals cannot hold their own in the world except by means of the reality principle. But this world is historically determined and is currently dominated by the demand for excessive production and forced consumption, the pursuit of better and better and more and more. The reality principle has, in other words, turned into the prevailing "performance principle." The performance principle is what unnecessarily and excessively oppresses humanity (EC 36).

These new categories of "performance principle" and "surplus repression" give us the proper view of Marcuse's dialectic of reason. Marcuse joins Freud in recognizing that human rationality is the rationality that the reality principle requires of humans and that there has of necessity always been something of repression in that rationality. Nowadays, however, it is this performance principle (rather than the reality principle from which it has grown) that gives birth to the rationality of modern society, and it is *surplus* repression that determines it. Scientific reason has delivered itself up to the performance principle. Science may well pretend that it respects only the facts, but these facts are the facts of the established social order, an order of performance and prestige.

Can we still speak of social "order"? Historical comparison shows that there has been a "qualitative change" in the culture and that order has degenerated into disorder. In modern rational civilization we face "growing irrationality." Is this a dialectic of enlightenment? Yes indeed, for the rationality of an order of necessary repression has swung around into the irrationality of a system of surplus repression that is neither necessary nor worthy of humanity. Yet this irrationality is not really obvious. Marcuse too discovers blindness everywhere. But the irrationality *can* be ascertained, once it is seen in historical perspective, in the light of a "higher rationality," i.e. in the light of a truly critical theory (EC 80).

Beyond (5)

Marcuse does not want to turn back the dialectic of civilization. It has to run its path to the very end. The dominance of the system, the alienation of work and the depersonalization of the individual in work must not be curbed, strange though it may sound. They must be completed. Going back to the past would mean going back to a world of scarcity, repressed desires and distorted personalities. The historical perspective points forwards not backwards. Paradise is shining ahead of us. "The elimination of human potentialities from the world of (alienated) labor creates the preconditions for the elimination of labor from the world of human potentialities" (EC 105). In other words, the inhuman world that has been created by the mechanization of work and the automation of work relationships is a realm of necessity that has no room for freedom but has in principle put an end to shortages of subsistence. This development was not foreseen by Freud, but it is the path that leads to a different, more humane world, the realm of freedom—even though the realm of work will remain necessary and will still have to support the realm of freedom.

What will this realm of freedom look like? In contrast to the other members of the Frankfurt School, Marcuse has, as we shall see in more detail in 4.3, put himself in an exceptionally vulnerable position by actually sketching in the outlines of the new reality. He starts by assuming that the new reality principle of performance and prestige has outlived itself, because it is nothing but the unpleasant outgrowth of the original reality principle. All that the reality principle did for humans was to lay down the conditions under which they could live with scarcity. As this scarcity is eliminated, so the reality principle itself can be dispensed with.

Marcuse has a vision of a new world society at the service of humankind. It is a society in which vital needs are no longer repressed but liberated, a society in which the reality principle and the pleasure principle can coincide. It is a utopian synthesis of libido and reality. It is the paradise of an eroticized culture, a paradise that Freud did not dare to dream of but that we may think of and work for.

In this new culture, claims Marcuse, humans will still have to let themselves be plugged into the automated production system, but this will be for no more than the minimum time necessary to furnish their needs, and it will certainly be possible to put a stop to extravagant *over*production. Apart from that, people will have a maximum of time and energy left over for enjoyment and pleasure, for play and fantasy, for creative work. Libido will no longer need to be repressed, nor will it have to be tied to sexual prowess and the reproductive urge within the confines of monogamy. It will be able to express itself in multiform sexuality, in the libidinous "cathexis" or investment of the entire human body, perhaps even in erotic-esthetic experiences of the entire objective world around us (EC 169).

This is not the place for a detailed analysis of Marcuse's vision of the future. This much is clear, that Marcuse sees in this prospect the concrete possibility of an eschatological reconciliation of all the oppositions that Freud had indicated in the culture. From the reconciliation of pleasure principle and reality principle, there follows the reconciliation of individual and society, of freedom and necessity, of fantasy and reason, of sensuousness and intellect, of matter and spirit. Indeed, perhaps even the life-impulse and the death-instinct can be reconciled—assuming that death can be interpreted in a non-repressive setting as the satiation of life and as "constant gratification" (EC 234).

Just as with Horkheimer and Adorno, Marcuse's vision of the future proves to be romantically colored. Marcuse sees himself here as one who stands in the romanticist tradition of men like Schiller (EC 180). He believes in an esthetic concept of culture in which spirit and matter are brought together into a higher unity as in a work of art, and in which the dialectical tension of art and repressive reason is abandoned and resolved in sensually and sensuously structured knowledge and in the cognitive power of imagination (EC 182, 149).

The paradise seems perfect. It *would* be perfect if it were not for that dualistic partner, the realm of harsh economic necessity. And if it were not for the scars, those painful reminders of the past. Let me therefore finish this chapter with the honest closing words of *Eros and Civilization*: "But even the ultimate advent of freedom cannot redeem those who died in pain. It is the remembrance of them, and the accumulated guilt of mankind against its victims, that darken the prospect of a civilization without repression" (EC 237).

4

The Political Marcuse

IN *EROS AND CIVILIZATION* (1956) Marcuse translated Freud's psychological and socio-psychological concepts into historical categories (EC 35). Afterwards, however, he reviews this interpretation. He argues then in the preface of the book that the Freudian concepts are essentially political categories—or, more accurately, that they have *become* political categories in modern industrial society. For it has to be realized that human consciousness and instinctual life are nowadays only an extension of totalitarian political power. Thus he states that the task is "to develop the political and sociological substance of the psychological notions."[1] Isn't this already a warning of the great gulf between dreams and political reality?

The One Dimensional Human (1)

Marcuse returns to this topic in the new edition of *Eros and Civilization* (1966). In the added "Political Preface" he frankly admits that his idea of the utopian union of eros and civilization was too optimistic and that he had grossly underestimated the gathering strength of the principle of performance and domination (EC xi). The awareness of the scourge of headlong economic development and of the manipulating powers in science and mass democracy appear to have completely changed his view of utopia. Liberation, he now says, is not only the most realistic of all historical possibilities but also the most repressed and the most remote

---

1. EC xxviii. See also Marcuse's "Freedom and Freud's Theory of Instincts" in which he suggests that the Freudian theory "which appears to be purely biological, is fundamentally social and historical." He sets out to show "to what extent the Freudian theory of instincts . . . makes it possible to understand the hidden nature of certain decisive tendencies in current politics," 1.

(EC xv). Society has been caught, not to say strangled, in the web of domination.

Marcuse directs his biting criticism not only at the totalitarian systems of world communism but also at the so-called free Western countries and in particular at the USA. At one time Marcuse favored America with a quotation from Hegel, calling it "the only land of the future."[2] Now he holds it up as a model of modern society, full of internal contradictions. America shows how production can be perverted into destruction, the welfare state into a warfare state and freedom into a system of domination.

Marcuse's diagnosis of modern culture resembles Horkheimer and Adorno's—but the therapy that he recommends certainly does not. It is typical of Marcuse that he responds to the current syndrome of modern society with activism, not pessimism. His language overflows with political agitation. The Freudian analysis of culture has to be politicized. What is required is a "juncture between the erotic and political dimension" (EC xxi). With "the great refusal"—a term borrowed from A.N. Whitehead—Marcuse originally meant to refer to the hidden truth of repressed instinct in art and fantasy (EC 149, 160). This refusal must now be organized and articulated in "intellectual refusal" (the scientists' and technicians' deliberate strike) and "instinctual refusal" (the instinctive protest of the young). What is needed today is thus a politicization of the truth that Freud had already announced. "Today the fight for life, the fight for Eros, is the *political* fight" (EC xxv).

Marcuse's most well-known book, *One Dimensional Man* (1964), continues in the spirit of *Eros and Civilization*. In the background there is still the Freudian theory of instincts with its pleasure principle and reality principle and its hypothesis of life instinct and death instinct (OM 72, 79). *One Dimensional Man*, however, begins where *Eros and Civilization* leaves off, with the modern welfare state that has moved into the center of the stage in the father role and has blotted out the individual's inner existence by constructing an automated superego, the socially conditioned conscience of the people.

What it boils down to is that the individual's laborious adaptation to reality via resentment, remorse, identification, and introjection is short-circuited in the political reality of today by immediate introjection, by automated assimilation, and by unconscious "mimesis" (in Horkheimer

---

2. Marcuse, *Reason and Revolution*, viii.

and Adorno's sense, OM 10). In this process, the inner, individual dimension of humans, as revealed in psychoanalysis, has been lost, even though this is really where the formation of the personal ego and of critical, negative thinking ought to take place. Only one dimension is left, that of socially streamlined man, one-dimensional in thought and behavior (OM 12). Hence the title of the book.

Freedom and "Project" (2)

What is new and valuable in *One Dimensional Man* is that Marcuse deals with the dialectic of reason on a more fundamental level than before. Originally he followed Freud in explaining reason and its repressive forms of expression in terms of the dynamics of the human instinctual mechanism in confrontation with a reality of scarce means. And he put forward repression-free reason as a historical alternative for the present on the basis of the newly acquired technical and industrial means to conquer this scarcity. Afterwards this possibility seemed to have been clouded over, because technical-industrial society had been cultivating repression and introjecting it directly into human consciousness. People are left only with political violence and a reinterpretation of today's society aimed at political violence.

Yet this political reinterpretation of present reality and the call to subjective refusal seemed to be no match for the objective tendencies of history. We might even wonder whether Marcuse really had freed himself from Freud's naturalistic mode of thought when he explained the repressiveness of reason, as far as the past is concerned, by the mechanism of human instincts and then, as far as the present is concerned, by the mechanism of social forces.

Thus in *One Dimensional Man* a turn in social policy is no longer made to depend on today's technological achievements in themselves. The whole of world history is now seen in a radical political perspective. In the past too, it is now said, humans faced social decisions. Then too the world of humans was their political option. Again and again humans stood at crossroads where, at a given level of knowledge and prosperity, they might have chosen any of the roads and where they themselves made the decision.

Marcuse was once a pupil of Heidegger and he uses Heidegger's and Sartre's existentialist, jargon. Thus he *calls* a historical act of choice, with all its consequences, a "project." By this term he wants to emphasize, as he himself puts it, the element of freedom and responsibility that humans have in a given contingent historical situation (OM xvi). For it is humans themselves that make a project of their world, even though such a project can subsequently, to a greater or lesser extent, start to live a life of its own and can make itself independent of those that "projected" it.

It is only at this point, in my estimation, that Marcuse really frees himself from Freud's naturalism and *learns* to say "no" in principle to the fatal drama of the dialectic of enlightenment. It does remain to be seen whether this principial "no" will stand or fall, but it is at any rate Marcuse's great virtue that he does not accept the doom of the cultural dialectic that has saddled us with this crazy conceited world. This dialectic is not doom. Humans themselves have willed their world from the start. Even today's technicized world was mapped out beforehand by human beings working from a particular idea, the idea of technological rationality (OM 123).

I consider this a crucial viewpoint.[3] Behind the *Aufklärung*'s technological and in principle totalitarian concept of *reason*, Marcuse sees free individuals, persons who are in principle responsible for this notion of reason. Too little notice has been taken of the fact that this way of seeing things determines the structure of *One Dimensional Man* and particularly underlies the second part. Here, technological reason is depicted as a particular project within the history of philosophy, a project that from the outset has stood in contrast to possible alternatives.

Marcuse wants to reduce the historical alternatives to a fundamental conflict between two types of rationality. On one side is the stabilizing force of so-called positive thinking that cannot do anything except re-

---

3. Nonetheless, we need to be cautious about statements to the effect that Marcuse more or less returned to the existentialism of his youth after the Second World War. (Such assertions can be found, for example, in J. Habermas's "Zum Geleit" and A. Schmidt's "Existential-Ontologie" in a volume edited by Habermas, *Antworten*, 13, 18.) In *Revolutionaire maatschappijkritiek* S.U.Zuidema rightly describes Marcuse as a neorationalist, even as a gnostic, who—quite unlike any existentialist—seeks salvation in the path of knowledge. Similar remarks could be made about the other members of the Frankfurt School (see 9.3 below). Moreover, in Marcuse true knowledge can be tested against the "universally valid standards" of vital human needs, although it may be that individuals cannot formulate these needs in a universally valid way unless they are in a state of freedom (OM 6). This universality is again quite contrary to the existentialist approach. Similarly, Habermas's consensus theory of truth anticipates that the universally human will emerge only in the ideal situation of unconstrained dialog (PKHI 79, KHI 284).

cord and check facts in the abstract enclosure of a law-governed world-picture. On the other side is the subversive power of negative, critical thinking that is not content with the facts, that is genuinely concerned at the fragmentation of this world, that exposes the world's contradictory tendencies, and that echoes and re-echoes Bloch's words "That which is cannot be true."[4]

In Marcuse's view this conflict was already brewing in the earliest history of thought. Even in Greek philosophy, subversive reason was already active (OM 167). The attitude of open critical enquiry in Plato's dialectical logic contrasted with the attitude of abstract organizing control in Aristotle's formal logic. Thus Plato and Aristotle are in Marcuse's eyes prototypes of what he would like to call the two-dimensional "logic of protest" versus the one-dimensional "logic of domination" (OM 123, 144).

Clearly, Marcuse sees himself and the Marxist theory of society as followers of the tradition of dialectical logic—a tradition in which in modern times he also includes thinkers like Hegel (OM 140). Equally obviously, Marcuse sees technological-totalitarian reason as an outgrowth of the tradition of formalized thinking. And it is this latter way of thinking that has established itself in the Western world since Galileo and Descartes—or one could say since the Renaissance and the Enlightenment.

Is Technology Politically Neutral? (3)

We will restrict ourselves to the above-mentioned contrast as it appears in modern times. Just as we did not dwell on Horkheimer's attempts to trace "aufklärerisch" thinking in the dim and distant past (1.1), so we will not get involved in Marcuse's attempts to hunt down the controversy of formal and critical thinking in ancient Greece. I make only the comment that such attempts seem to me not to do justice to the discontinuity and diversity of history nor, more particularly, to the newness and uniqueness of the modern period, which has most of its roots in the spiritual climate of the Renaissance and the Enlightenment.[5]

What is of importance for Marcuse's view is that when the abstract analytical thinking of the Western sciences is seen in historical perspective, it proves to be no more than a particular project—not something

---

4. OM 123. See Bloch, *Philosophische Grundfragen*, vol.1, 65.
5. See Klapwijk, *Tussen historisme en relativisme*, 1–28. See 9.2 below.

that thinking foists on humankind but something that human beings actually opt for. For scientific reason develops under a "technological *a priori.*" The natural sciences are committed *in advance* to examining and illuminating nature as material to be dominated and as an instrument to dominate with. And because this intervention in nature sooner or later, directly or indirectly, means intervention in human life, the technological *a priori* is essentially a political *a priori* (OM 153–54). In other words, not even the most abstract theory of physics is divorced from questions of social responsibility.

Here Marcuse is, I think, more radical than his colleagues in Frankfurt. He challenges not only the neutrality of science but even the neutrality of technology.[6] Technology can never be viewed apart from its practical and political applications: "The traditional notion of the 'neutrality' of technology can no longer be maintained" (OM xvi). The principle of domination does not just extend itself by means of technology, it expands *as* technology. When all is said and done, the power of the machine is the incarnate power of humans themselves (OM 158, 3).

So modern technical and scientific progress does have political aspirations (OM 233). A revolution could not achieve anything except "to the degree to which it would alter the direction of technical progress—that is, develop a new technology" (OM 227). A new society means the collapse of the current scientific "project" and the development of a new technology, a new concept of theoretical and practical rationality, and a new structure of science (OM 228, 166).

In the new order, reason will no longer be allowed to suppress nature, including human nature, in the sense of technological exploitation. Nor will it be allowed simply to extol nature in the sense of romanticist idolization. No, the technology that Marcuse is aiming at will have to elevate nature, free it from its blindness and brutishness, and place it in the framework of a pacified existence conceived in esteticist terms along the lines of *Eros and Civilization* (OM 236). To this end, the present gulf that divides the rationality of science and technology from the irrationality of art and fantasy ought to be bridged in an esteticization and politiciza-

---

6. OM 154f. Marcuse's appeal to Marx seems to me unjustifiable (see 6.1). There are other places in which Marcuse denies the neutrality of technology: "Technology is always a historical-social project: in it is projected what a society and its ruling interests intend to do with men and things" or, again, "as 'congealed spirit', the machine is not neutral," in "Industrialization," 224–25.

tion of reason (OM 228, 234). This new type of reason could create and promote the "Good Life" in a new and more humane world (OK 230).

Marcuse himself undermines his own idea of a new rationality when, as in *Eros and Civilization*, he ultimately does build the kingdom of freedom, peace, and direct democracy on top of the harsh realm of necessity, an inevitable infrastructure in society characterized by mechanized labor and centralized production planning and food distribution. It may well be that exploitation and overproduction get short shrift in this new kingdom, but technological rationality is still there as "the sole standard and guide in planning and developing the available resources for all" (OM 251). As far as I can see, this technology cannot mean anything but a politically neutral, or at least neutralized, technology, a basic provision with no room for free projects or human choice. In other words, free self-determination can only be realized in the technical-rational management of "the economic surplus" (OM 252).

It seems fair here to speak of an inconsistency in Marcuse.[7] But any utopia is ultimately open to attack, and whether Marcuse is inconsistent or not, he has at least seen more clearly than others that *if* technology is getting out of hand, *if* science is tyrannizing us, then this cannot simply be reduced to a matter of the dialectic of reason. Behind the dialectic lurks something else. Is it a construction fault in the human organism? Is it a bottleneck in human instinctual life? Marcuse's reply in *One Dimensional Man* is that what is hiding behind the dialectic is human freedom and responsibility. Throughout the whole of history humans are fundamentally accountable for their actions, even in terms of science and technology.

Sadly, Marcuse leaves us in the lurch so far as the position of modern humanity is concerned. Humankind in our time is his view so cocooned in the technical-scientific complex that freedom and liberation have become an illusion. Freedom is won by criticizing the authorities. The greater the array of power, the fiercer is the opposition and the more intense the urge for liberation. That is the dialectical pattern of history, the inexorable swing from suppression to liberation. Marcuse puts his faith in this liberating dialectic.[8] But what if the power of the authorities has become totalitarian? Then it is also able to smother all criticism. In fact this power can even manipulate the urge for liberty to its own ends. Freedom itself becomes a tool of domination (OM 7).

7. Compare Habermas, TW 58ff., TRS 88ff.
8. Marcuse, "Liberation," 175.

The Vicious Circle (4)

We come now to the crux of Marcuse's version of the critical theory. How can the aspiration for freedom find its way into a world that has become totalitarian, a world of one-dimensional people? Marcuse himself sees a vicious circle here.[9] "How can the people who have been the object of effective and productive domination by themselves create the conditions of freedom" (OM 6)? For there is no conceivable way that people can work for liberty as long as they live in a world that is able to manipulate them even in their longing for freedom (OM 253). "The slaves must be *free for* their liberation before they can become free" (OM 41). In other words, "we have to be free in order to create a free society."[10] What is behind these statements is not just the practical problem of whether there are any revolutionaries left, it is a problem of principle: "How is it even thinkable that the vicious circle be broken" (OM 251)?

Marcuse has uncovered a weak spot in today's critical social theory, "the point of its greatest weakness." In earlier Marxist theory, criticism of society was assumed to take off from the objective and subjective factors in history that were moving towards liberation. Consider for example, the objectivity of economic crises or the subjectivity of revolutionary proletarian consciousness. Marcuse maintains that such "inherent possibilities" (OM 255) no longer exist in the established and self-consolidating order of the modern "System." Thus critical thought has to be content with theoretical explanation of the facts and theoretical exposure of the contradictions that are bottled up within the facts. In this way critical thought can create what Hegel used to call a "definite" or "determinate negation" ("bestimmte Negation") and what Marcuse prefers for clarity's sake to call a "determinate choice" (OM 221). Although the choice that critical thought makes is necessarily determined by and within historical development, the act of choice is nevertheless the free project of a different reality. By virtue of this, the choice negates what is given (OM 219). Marcuse calls this, in line with Hegelian historicist thinking, "the ingression of liberty into historical necessity."[11]

Marcuse is well aware that such a choice remains theoretical and utopian. It does not contain any positive and practical chance, because

---

9. OM 223, *Dialectics of Liberation*, 178.
10. *Dialectics of Liberation*, 186.
11. OM 221. Compare Klapwijk, *Tussen historisme en relativisme*, 40.

practice simply does not heed the call of theory any more. So theory can say what ought *not* to be done, but no longer what *ought* to be done. Dialectical theory in our day remains of necessity a negative theory (OM 253). And that comes pretty close to a self-condemnation when judged in the light of Marx's famous dictum: "Philosophers have only *interpreted* the world in various ways; the point is to *change* it."[12]

For this reason, Marcuse makes a desperate attempt, at the end of *One Dimensional Man* and elsewhere, to launch a program of action out of—or rather in opposition to—the dead-end of historical development. His language is garnished with political sentiment. An "essentially new historical Subject" must emerge (OM 252), one that is not prepared to compromise in the slightest but *is* prepared to go to extremes—to "absolute refusal," to a "total rupture" with established society.[13] If practical and material resistance can no longer rise up from inside, then it may have to come from outside, from the far corners of the earth. The outcasts will rise up—the blacks, the unemployed, the underdeveloped—spewed out of the mouth of that modern Mammon-Moloch, Big Business.

And these revolutionary outcasts must be supported by the revolutionary consciousness of those that are critical and not yet totally corrupted, the youth. Let there be a conspiracy of those that have been spewed out and those that have not yet been digested. The earth's rejects have clenched their fists in blind rage. The light of critical reason must direct them to the ironclad walls of the System. Power against power. And for all that, history is a dead-end that allows no sure view of a road that might lead to success. "It is nothing but a chance" (OM 257).

This practical program of Marcuse's—quite apart from the uncertainty of its outcome—does not really escape from that weakness of the critical theory that we have already mentioned. Elsewhere Marcuse has said that all dialectic is liberation from a repressive system and liberation "by forces developing within such a system . . . by virtue of the contradiction generated by the system, precisely because it is a bad, a false

---

12. "Die Philosophen haben die Welt nur verschieden *interpretiert*; es kommt darauf an, sie zu *verändern*." In Marx, "Thesen über Feuerbach," XI.

13. The term "the Great Refusal," taken from Whitehead, originally referred to the secret message of the repressed instinct which was conveyed in the language of art (see 4.1 above). In *One Dimensional Man* it becomes the political parole for critical students and fringe groups (OM 63, 64), indeed for all who have suffered for the truth (OM 257). For the term "total rupture," see *Dialectics of Liberation*, 177.

system."[14] As a dialectical theory, the critical theory can take account only of internal possibilities, not of possibilities from outside. Such external possibilities—if they did indeed come from outside and were not the product of a shared destiny—could only be interpreted as a violent authoritarian invasion. In short, the practical solution offered in *One Dimensional Man* is an emergency measure, and one that is at odds with the basic ideas of Neo-Marxism.

Reviewing Marcuse, I cannot help concluding that we are still confronted with the vicious circle he discovered in his own theory. If the so-called dialectic of enlightenment has landed us in a totally controlled world, how is it possible to be liberated from it? Who is to liberate the liberators? Who can create even the basic conditions for revolutionary resistance? Earlier on we saw how Horkheimer and his associates expressed their extreme skepticism about the possibility of real revolutionary campaigning. However much Marcuse may have stepped forward as the prophet of the student revolutionary movement, the question nevertheless arises whether the net result of his thinking is not precisely what Horkheimer was afraid of.

There is actually a further problem with Marcuse's ideas. His thinking not only leads us to wonder about the material resistance of revolutionary groups, it also puts a question mark against the spiritual resistance of critical thinking itself. If both deeds and thoughts, both language and theory, are being manipulated in the modern enterprise of consciousness-management, then is not the critical theory itself deprived of its very basis of existence? We have already asked whether someone who is being manipulated can be a revolutionary. We must now ask whether someone who is being manipulated can even be critical. It was Adorno in particular who saw this second quandary and who tackled it in his *Negative Dialectics*.

---

14. The quotation is from *Dialectics of Liberation*, 175. Here Marcuse goes on to emphasize two things: On the one hand he stresses the disintegration *within* the established order (180) and the *internal* resistance by students, provos and hippies (190). On the other hand he refers to the broader framework within which the West stands over against the Third World and the centers of resistance which he presumes exist there (191). On this global scale Marcuse can perhaps still talk about "inherent possibilities"— but then the world he is describing is less totalitarian than the Frankfurt School would have us believe. Elsewhere, in an essay entitled "Zum Begriff der Negation," Marcuse himself speaks of the "questionable" nature of the dialectic of the negation, which is supposed to "unfold as liberation *within* an existing whole." See Marcuse, *Ideen*, 188, and section 9.3 of this book.

5

Adorno and the Negative Dialectic

ADORNO'S PRINCIPAL WORK IS *Negative Dialektik* (1966, English translation *Negative Dialectics*, 1973). Ingenious but abstract, this book is dominated by the notion of the dialectic of enlightenment and its possible consequences for critical thought. "As far back as we can trace it, the history of thought has been a dialectic of enlightenment" (NDcs 118; "Die Geschichte des Denkens ist, soweit sie irgend sich zurückverfolgen läßt, Dialektik der Aufklärung," ND 122). This universal *Aufklärung*, Adorno has to note, has not brought progress but rather regression. "No universal history leads from savagery to humanitarianism, but there is one leading from the slingshot to the megaton bomb." Hegel's expectation that world history would one day be dominated by reasonableness is horrifyingly verified—in a world that is indeed *dominated* by reason (ND 312, NDcs 320).

Humankind Died in Auschwitz (1)

Dominating reason has become powerful by building up the appearance of total "identity" between the concept and that which is conceived of. It is as if anything that is conceptualized is thereby totally absorbed into the concept. Thinking seems to be nothing other than apprehending and comprehending the world. The thing is completely assimilated into the concept. "To think is to identify" (NDcs 5; "Denken heißt identifizieren" ND 15).

This principle of identification is not just some innocent fact of life. On the contrary, by assuming that universal conceptual structures and concrete reality are identical, thinking is busily exercising its mastery over the material it is dealing with (ND 30, NDcs 21–22). The more so because to identify is also to systematize, an exercise *and* extension of power. As a consequence, things are smoothed out to fit conceptual structure, qualitative moments are flattened out (ND 93, NDcs 88), and objects are consistently quantified and cataloged. Above all, thinking underrates human subjectivity. It has objectified human beings and rammed them into the abstract universal pigeon-holes of concept, system, and organization (ND 29, NDcs 20).

The most horrible result of this strategy was Auschwitz. Auschwitz! For Adorno the word has a metaphysical meaning, a special revelatory value. It was not until Auschwitz that it became really plain just how far the degradation of humanity has gone in modern history. Auschwitz was where human beings finally lost their last pathetic possession, their very individuality. Particular individuals did not die there, it was humankind. Those that died were odd anonymous specimens of the human species (ND 353, NDcs 362), standardized items to be counted and controlled.

According to Adorno, the process of identifying and systematizing has a counterpart in the social order (ND 32, NDcs 23). The identification principle has been grafted on to the exchange principle, which long ago standardized and totalized the production of goods, hidden behind a diversity of trademarks (ND 93, 147, 175, NDcs 88–89, 146, 176). In Adorno's argument, present-day *Herrschaft* or domination therefore draws its energy from the general principle of identity, totality, and equivalence, a principle that erases individual differences and that has put the entire world under the spell of the identifying concept (ND 178, NDcs 180). Myth has come to life again in a concept fetishism ("Begriffsfetischismus"). What Marx called the "fetishism of commodities" was only one outgrowth of this more general fetishism (ND 56, NDcs 52). The concept grasps the whole and thereby grasps thin air: "The whole is the false."[1] In other words, the whole is a mystification: "The *totum* is the totem" (ND 368, NDcs 377).

In opposition to the prevailing omnipotence of identifying thought, Adorno puts forward the need for dialectic thought. Dialectic is not a matter of mere methodology, but no more is it a pure ontic reality. Dialectic is not pure logic or method, because its method is a method of contradiction evoked by contradictions and conflicts in reality itself. But neither is dialectic purely ontic, a simple reality, because the actual contradictions in reality are not immediately obvious from the facts and cannot be assessed and refuted unless confronted by thinking. Dialectical thinking is thus thinking that contradicts the contradiction

1. Adorno, *Minima Moralia*, § 29.

discovered in reality itself. It is a saying "no" to the existing ambivalence and non-identity of the world (ND 145, 56, NDcs 144–45, 52–53). "Dialectics is the consistent sense of nonidentity" (NDcs 5; "Dialektik ist das konsequente Bewußtsein von Nichtidentität" ND 15).

By virtue of this, dialectical thinking attacks unity thinking and identity thinking, for unitarian thinking and identitarian thinking use logical systematics to paper over the cracks in reality. Today's dialecticians will thus have to carry their thinking through more rigorously than their predecessors, more even than Hegel, that dialectician par excellence. Even though *Negative Dialectics* seems at first sight to be strongly oriented to Hegel, more so than to Marx, Adorno does not acquiesce in Hegel's wish to capture the dialectic in the synthetic unity of the logical subject (in what Hegel called "the identity of identity and nonidentity," ND 17,158, NDcs 7, 153–59). Putting it more simply, Hegel too ends up with the negative drive of the dialectic resulting in something positive. It seems as though minus times minus will just have to make a plus. But Adorno doubts very much whether humankind's "no" to a world that says "no" to humankind yields anything positive (ND 7, NDcs xx). Hegel's positive outcome of world history—and Marx's too for that matter—gives Adorno the impression that the conceptualizing subject is yet again showing its accursed urge to identify (ND 143, NDcs 142).

Now we can understand why Adorno gave his book the bizarre title of *Negative Dialectics*. Through all the laborious twists in the book, the reader must catch the strains of a declaration of solidarity—theory affirming its solidarity with the agony of practice, theory refusing to turn its eyes towards the positive and away from a world bleeding from a thousand wounds. Since Auschwitz, the world has shown its true colors in its "absolute negativity." To try to wring some positive sense out of this world is to betray its victims (ND 352, NDcs 361). Adorno's dialectic is negative because it radically mistrusts anything that is conceived positively and because it cannot help turning to what the concept misses or resists. For this reason Adorno says "To change this direction of conceptuality, to give it a turn toward nonidentity, is the hinge of negative dialectics" (ND 22, NDcs 12).

Thinking and Suffering (2)

At this point we come right up against the distress of dialectical thinking. The trouble with philosophy is that it is "forced to operate with concepts"

(ND 21, NDcs 11). For, if the dialectic of enlightenment boils down to the corruption of the concept, this corruption cannot be recognized except in concepts, i.e. by corrupt means. "Even the self-critical turn of unitarian thinking depends on concepts..." (ND 158, NDcs 158).

No wonder that Adorno talks of philosophy as the urge to "express the inexpressible" to itself (ND 113, NDcs108). Philosophy is really notionless. It faces the impossible task of surmounting the concept via the concept. "It must strive, by way of the concept, to transcend the concept" (NDcs 15; "über den Begriff durch den Begriff hinauszugelangen," ND 25). It must so to speak be able to jump over its own shadow. For philosophy is concerned with reality in its otherness, in its fullness. But how can this reality be imagined without conceptual images or representations? (ND 205, NDcs 207) "Philosophy, like music, is at a loss to express itself" (ND 43, NDcs 33).

At the same time this tells us why critical theorists following Adorno's line are reluctant to map out the future of humankind and society. A design of the future such as Marcuse tries to give in *Eros and Civilization* does not just run into practical problems but meets principled resistance. The more realistic such a utopia and the more concrete such an anthropology, the more deceptive they are. In fact if you start to visualize humans and their future potential on the basis of the current circumstances and prevailing concepts, you are *identifying* the future and thus sabotaging it (ND 128, NDcs 130). Hence the "ineffable" character of the utopia (ND 20, NDcs 11).

The negative dialectic itself shows traces of the damnable identification principle. The dialectic may formulate a contradiction to oppose the counterfeit unity and identity of conceptual conformity, but this contradiction is nevertheless tied to the basic concepts of the "identitarian philosophy" that is being criticized and to that extent is itself false (ND 148, NDcs 147). Indeed, as far as Adorno is concerned, the very method of contradiction is open to challenge, for it is actually a violation of the rules of formal logic—as long as we don't forget that this method is evoked and incited by identity thinking itself (ND 16, NDcs 6–7).

This means that the negative dialectic comes to us as an "anti-system," searching as it is for what lies outside the sway of the unity principle (ND 8, NDcs xx). The anti-system is not rigid but creative. Like Marcuse's alternative thinking, it is playful and speculative (ND 24, 25, NDcs 14, 15). Thus the negative dialectic finds its engaging force not in systematically worked out argumentation but in models of thought. "The call for binding statements without a system is a call for thought models" (ND37, NDcs 29). The only way to reflect on being and existence, freedom, history, and the metaphysical-absolute is in models (ND 146, 207, NDcs 146, 209). So it is that Adorno can define the negative dialectic as "an ensemble of analyses of models" (NDcs 27; "ein Ensemble von Modellanalysen," ND 37).

One might be inclined to say that such a way of thinking, which operates on the fringes of totalizing unity thinking and which aims to think and interpret that which is really neither thinkable nor expressible, is highly subjective. But Adorno believes that these subjective attempts at expression are based on a colossal objectivity that is unmistakable even under the sway of domination. It is the objectivity of suffering.

Dialectical thinking is related to suffering, which seeks escape and expression, just as suffering is related to dialectic, which alone discerns and verbalizes it as suffering. "The need to lend a voice to suffering is a condition of all truth. For suffering is objectivity that weighs upon the subject" (ND 27, NDcs 17–18). In other words the objective legitimation of philosophy lies in suffering—however much philosophy may for the rest turn out to be hopelessly subjective. "Perennial suffering has as much right to expression as a tortured man has to scream" (ND 353, NDcs 362). Just as Adorno finds the inarticulate groaning of the tortured vastly more truthful than the sweetly phrased language of culture, so he infinitely prefers the expressionistic rhetoric of the dialectic to the antiseptic linguistic protocol of normal science (ND 63, NDcs 56).

Materialism and Maturity (3)

We said earlier that Adorno's stress on a consistent dialectic of reason made him a close follower of Hegel. Yet it would be highly misleading to let this statement stand without some drastic qualifications. Adorno wants to follow the path of the *Aufklärung* and its quest for rational and responsible maturity.[2] But Adorno does not believe that reason is a sovereign independent subject. He believes rather that it has its roots

---

2. Translators' Note: German *Mündigkeit* (Dutch *mondigheid*) means "majority" in the sense of having reached the age of legal responsibility, but the word must also be understood against the background of its use by Kant. In an attempt to convey this sense, Shapiro translates "autonomy and responsibility" (KHI 342). Here and subsequently we have preferred the more direct term "maturity."

in the objectivity of bodily nature and suffering. It is this "primacy" or "preponderance" of the object ("Vorrang des Objekts," ND 182–83, NDcs 183–84) that does after all shift Adorno's dialectical theory away from the subjectivism of Hegelian idealism. The negative dialectic is a critique of human and social suppression, based on solidarity with the oppressed. In that sense it has a Marxist and materialist character.

This materialism, however, should be understood not so much in an economic sense as in a physical or "somatic" sense (ND 191, NDcs 193). The critique is not prompted by solidarity with the working class, for the working class is not only a victim but also an accomplice of the "domination system." It is more reminiscent of Marcuse's critique (3.5) and of Horkheimer and Adorno's earlier work (2.2), a critique that springs from a sense of solidarity with oppressed nature and oppressed human life, wherever they are found and in whatever form they appear.

Unlike Marx's materialism and certainly unlike Lenin's,[3] Adorno's is definitely not naïve, i.e. based on an uncritical epistemology. From what we have already said about Adorno's conception of dialectics it is plain that ontic reality and the suffering encountered in it do not just exist of their own accord but are dependent on the articulating power of critical reason. Despite this, persistent reflection will reveal that reason itself ultimately lives from a somatic impulse: "All mental things are modified physical impulses" (NDcs 202; "Alles Geistige ist modifiziert leibhafter Impuls," ND 200). And the glaring deficiency of identity thinking, including Hegel's, is that it reduces what is material to an object for a subject and ignores the fact that the subject itself is basically also an object (ND 182, NDcs 183). The dialectic of enlightenment remains in darkness until the critical light penetrates to the affinity of mind and matter, and thinking comes to understand its affinity with the bodily realm. Indeed, this is what Horkheimer and Adorno had already proposed in their original conception. In the same spirit it is now said that "affinity is the point of a dialectics of enlightenment" (NDcs 270; "Affinität ist die Spitze einer Dialektik von Aufklärung," ND 264).

Nevertheless the pitfall in this materialist interpretation of the negative dialectic is clear enough. Anyone who accepts the affinity of mind and matter as if it were directly and intuitively obvious—think for example of the romanticism of Schelling or Schiller—is indulging in

---

3. Lenin, *Materialism and Empirio-Criticism*, 143ff. For further comments on Marx, see 7.2 below.

what Adorno calls the "rehashed myth" ("aufgewärmte Mythe"), the dish that the dialectic of enlightenment has already been serving up for far too long. Adorno's view is that we have to fight our way through to this affinity, breaking the spell of existence and penetrating the 'mimicry' of thinking with the weapon of criticism (ND 264–65, NDcs 269–70).

In other words, we must not slide back into the myth of mother nature. What is needed instead of this all too common retreat is for the enlightenment to transcend itself in a "progressively enlightened mind" (NDcs 269; "fortschreitende Aufklärung," ND 264). There is need "for subjective reflection, and for reflection on the subject" (NDcs 185; "Selbstreflexion der Aufklärung," ND 184). There is no prospect in the way in which humans used to be mythically enslaved to nature, nor is there in the current domination of nature by humans which, when you get down to brass tacks, is really another form of mythical enslavement anyway. A prospect is in the human being's concentrating on the self, a process that can eventually merge into a process of humans' finding their way back to nature. This is what Adorno is getting at when he says that "enlightenment is 'demythologization'—no longer merely as *reductio ad hominem* but the other way round, as a *reductio hominis*" (ND 185, NDcs 186).

Perhaps we can state it as follows. Adorno wants to go further along the path of the *Aufklärung* and its quest for responsible maturity. But it can no longer be a matter of striving to be responsible over against nature but rather to be responsible and responding from within nature. Humans speak *for* nature. Like an exhaust valve, they give vent to nature's intolerable tensions.

The Approaching Catastrophe (4)

Philosophy has precious little room to maneuver. The freedom of philosophy is no more than the ability to put its lack of freedom into words (ND 27, NDcs 18). If there were no repression, one could not even conceive of freedom, let alone achieve it (ND 260, NDcs 265). Yet one cannot cling to freedom of thinking and the possibility of criticism unless one assumes that the prevailing bondage is *not* a result of immutable destiny. On the historical level, seen from the perspective of historical necessity, this bondage can indeed be said to be inevitable, but at a deeper level it is not intrinsically necessary. Everything in this world *could* have been different. If criticism is still to have meaning, the things that are historically necessary must be metaphysically accidental.

How is it that things can be accidental? Right from the start of the journey, the train must have been on the wrong track. Adorno surmises that some "irrational catastrophe" in the beginning lies behind the catastrophe that is to come. Ever since that first catastrophe, hopes for a new world have been frustrated. Nonetheless our task is still one of "averting catastrophe in spite of everything" (ND 315, NDcs 323). We might wonder here whether the dialectical criticism does not come close to a conservative desire to keep things the way they are. Is there a suggestion here that we should anticipate the coming disaster by being careful to preserve what little we have in the way of freedoms and possibilities of thinking?

Here we come to the question of the relationship between critical theory and revolutionary practice. Although Adorno, in good Marxist fashion, holds in principle to the unity of theory and practice, he does put more stress than he used to on the fact that their interrelationship varies down through history and that they are currently far apart from each other (ND 144–45, NDcs 143–44; see 2.3 above). On one side is practice, in which repugnance and impatience can be found, but only in vague stirrings. On the other side is the critical idea, which sees into the why and wherefore of the repugnant injustice, but which is powerless to intervene (ND 279–80, NDcs 285–86).

Since revolutionary practice has been blocked for the time being, thinking has a chance to catch its breath. Reason must go into hibernation. Circumstances are forcing reason into the good fortune of contemplation and pure intellectual work ("the happy spirit," NDcs 245, "Glück am Geist," ND 241). It is soon apparent that this is nevertheless a dubious sort of good fortune, since theory is also affected by stranded practice. Really the only ones for whom happiness is still in store are people that are no longer themselves, those that can either live with the burden of self-alienation or that sink under it into schizophrenia.[4]

Does Adorno still believe, as he once did (2.2), in the possibility of a reconciled world in which suffering has disappeared and mind and

---

4. ND 275, NDcs 280. I think Rohrmoser is misleading when he claims that Adorno describes schizophrenia as today's "way to salvation" and "true form of subjectivity" (*Elend der kritischen Theorie*, 32). Elsewhere Adorno expressly says that "involuntary ataraxy" (a life of passive contemplation or indifference) and "bestiality" are "wrong ways of living" (NDcs 364; "falsches Leben," ND 354).

matter are united? Looking at history, with its massive surge of necessity, we have to answer no. At any rate, the vision of Hegel, Marx, and Engels that freedom boils down to insight into historical necessity certainly rests on a false notion of reconciliation.[5] Adorno does occasionally mention positive reconciliation, but only as "Sehnsucht," as hope and longing (ND 150, NDcs 150). Those famous words of Walter Benjamin, the lonely pioneer of the Frankfurt School, already expressed what is in Adorno's heart: "For the sake of the hopeless only are we given hope" (NDcs 378; "Nur um der Hoffnungslosen willen ist uns die Hoffnung gegeben," ND 369).

The Hope Principle (5)

Oddly enough, this hope is mentioned at the end of *Negative Dialectics* where it has only now become apparent just how hopeless the essential state of the critical theory is. If Marcuse showed how the totalitarian system threatened liberating practice, then Adorno has shown how greatly it is endangering the critical theory as well. And on all fronts too. For now it has become clear that the theory is purely negative; it must draw its life from criticism. It is equally clear that the theory is impractical; it has to hibernate as pure theory. Finally it is also plain that the theory is corrupt; it is tainted by the very practice that it criticizes.

So there can be no talk of hope unless the theory is utterly consistent and turns against itself. Theory has to perform major surgery on its own person. "To this end, dialectics is obliged to make a final move: being at once the impression and the critique of the universal delusive context, it must now turn even against itself" (NDcs 406; "Dazu muß Dialektik, in eins Abdruck des universalen Verblendungszusammenhang und dessen Kritik, in einer letzten Bewegung sich noch gegen sich selbst kehren" ND 395). Its objective aim then becomes a "negation of the negation" of the world's negativity, i.e. criticism of the critical theory. The theory's concepts are traitors within thinking's domain and criticism must try to defeat them with similar weapons. It must engage its own concepts in conceptual combat. In that way it can hope to get outside itself and manage to catch a glimpse of the absolute that lives beyond the spell of identity (ND 396, NDcs 406), the absolute that Horkheimer calls "the totally other" ("das ganz Andere," 8.2). Enlightenment may have swung around

---

5. ND 244; NDcs 248. For comments on Marx and Engels in the context of their Hegelian background, see O'Rourke, *Problem of Freedom*, 38f., 55f., etc.

into the universal blindness of the concept, but if the conceptual blanket can unpick its own threads, there may yet be an opening of hope.

Negative dialectics thus becomes a metaphysics (not a theology!) of hope.[6] In this it can be compared with Ernst Bloch's "philosophy of hope." As in Bloch, the dialectic is carried along by yearning ("Sehnsucht"). This *Sehnsucht* provides the motive for the striving, mentioned earlier, to transcend the concept by way of the concept (ND 25, NDcs15). It is a materialist longing that strives not for a clear self-conception of the spirit, as Hegel did, but—to use a tentative expression (ND 369, NDcs 378)—for what theologians call "the resurrection of the flesh." The complete object cannot be grasped in a conceptual image or representation just as theology in its own way forbids images or representations of God. The object of *Sehnsucht* must rather be sounded or fathomed, and then only when the bodily impulse has been allayed and the spirit can be reconciled to it (ND 205, NDcs 208). This idea of Adorno's might almost coincide with Marcuse's romanticist vision of the future (3.5), if only it were not so bitterly suspicious of itself and the future.

All in all, this metaphysics of hope is tottering on the brink of despair. Metaphysical experience jumps into the breach where life perishes in hopelessness. And, in so doing, it desperately searches for a way out. "It is impossible to think of death as the last thing pure and simple" - yet there is no guarantee of the notion of a hereafter (ND 362, NDcs 371-72). Thinking can fumble towards that which is "other" and "incommensurable"—yet nowhere is there anything to support the idea of the absolute (ND 395, NDcs 405).

The Aufklärung has repressed metaphysics as the philosophy of ultimate unity. Metaphysics can now function only in a fragmentary way, as a model, as a "micrology," as a science of minute differences (ND 397, NDcs 407). It can function only by paying careful attention to any minute item that breaks the spell of existence in being critically elucidated and in its uniqueness lights up for a moment and points towards the absolute.

---

6. Adorno would not be willing to talk of a "theology of hope." Metaphysics is not theology, not even secularized theology, but criticism of theology, criticism which uncovers "the possibility of what theology may force upon men and thus desecrate" (ND 387, MDcs 397). Thus in Adorno's eyes, theology is authoritarian, whereas metaphysics is in principle autonomous. In this respect the Frankfurt School once again show themselves to be true heirs of the *Aufklärung*: Any notion of divine authority would be a violation of human maturity. See further 9.3, 9.4.

Metaphysics naturally encompasses something of longing and need, but does that make it a projection? Isn't such *Sehnsucht* (Habermas would call it "emancipatory interest," 7.5) also the deepest impulse of thinking itself? If so, critical thinking is in sympathy with this metaphysics. For what is involved is not the (imagined) image of expectations and desires, but hope that clings to the tokens of criticism. It is as if criticism manages to chip marks on the granite mass that this world has become. For an instant, these marks may yet fall into place as the hieroglyphs of the absolute. So Adorno concludes "There is solidarity between such thinking and metaphysics at the time of its fall" (NDcs 408; "Solches Denken ist solidarisch mit Metaphysik im Augenblick ihres Sturzes," ND 398).

Adorno's *Negative Dialectics* is a courageous book, but written with the courage of desperation. The dialectic of enlightenment has almost completely overclouded thinking. There is scarcely enough light for criticism even to see how massive the cloud is. There are only brief glimpses of a different world.

6

Habermas and Technocratic Ideology

THE HEAVINESS THAT READERS can almost feel choking them in *Negative Dialectics* can be understood only in the context of Adorno's view of the dialectic of enlightenment. To Adorno, reason is not just ambivalent, it is intrinsically corrupt. To think is to identify, to dominate, to oppress. Are these equations of Adorno's really justifiable?

Not according to Jürgen Habermas.[1] In the 1960s a younger generation came to the forefront in the Frankfurt School and Habermas is perhaps the most representative among them. Habermas combines harsh criticism of society in the spirit of Marcuse with radical criticism of knowledge in the spirit of Adorno. In fact (as we shall see in 7.4) he considers that radical criticism of knowledge is thinkable and feasible only as criticism of society.

Technology and Science as Ideology (1)

Habermas's criticism is still inspired by the theme of the dialectic of enlightenment, even though it may be expressed less explicitly than in Adorno's work. Habermas recognizes that scientific reason has been remythologized when he observes that Westerners have made a "fetish" of science (TW 89, TRS 111). Especially in the social sciences, humans are under the spell of an "illusion" and as a result are at the mercy of the "revenge" of the object.[2] For this reason Habermas is extremely

---

1. Habermas, born in Gummersbach in 1929, was first Adorno's *Assistent* and then in 1964 succeeded Horkheimer as professor of philosophy and sociology at the University of Frankfurt. In 1971 he became director of the Max Planck Institute for Research into the Life Conditions of the Scientific and Technical World in Starnberg.

2. Habermas, "Analytische Wissenschaftstheorie," 191, 158; English translation: "Analytical Theory," 162, 134.

suspicious of Western rationality, which, he says, shows a "Janus face," "dichotomy," and "ambiguity" (TRS 83, 89, 415; "ihr doppeltes Gesicht," "Zwiespältigkeit," "Zweideutigkeit," TW 51, 59, 94).

One of Habermas's most instructive publications on this point is "Technology and Science as 'Ideology.'" In it he acknowledges that the ambiguity he is talking about is the same thing that Horkheimer and Adorno had already recognized as the "dialectic of enlightenment." According to him, Marcuse had later specified this dialectic by claiming that Western science and technology had gradually turned into an ideology.[3] Habermas thus comes to the formula that is the title of his essay: "technology and science as ideology."[4]

This formula can be said to be the mold in which Habermas recasts the theme of the dialectic of enlightenment. Habermas is certainly closely related to his predecessors in the Frankfurt School, but, when the formula is elaborated, he also presents certain points of difference from them, even from Marcuse, to whom he makes his initial appeal.

Habermas shares Marcuse's opinion that the process of "rationalization" that has been going on in modern society for centuries is usually described too formally, especially by Max Weber. Weber maintained that this rationalization was really just a direct consequence of the consistent human pursuit of rational goals and the use of technical ingenuity in all sectors of society, accompanied by decaying cultural values and a less and less authoritative world-view. But Marcuse, according to Habermas, showed beyond all doubt that much more was involved—that anonymous forms of political power were increasingly dominating society under the cloak of rationalization. This power was simply hiding behind a facade of so-called expertise and technical efficiency.

We have seen earlier that Marcuse consequently disputed the neutrality of science and technology and began to think about an alternative reason, a different conception of science, a new technology. But we also noted that Marcuse himself still stuck to a rather matter-of-fact notion of technical rationality and mechanical labor. This was especially evident in the way he talked about the realm of harsh objective necessity that left

---

3. TW 49, TRS 82. Here Habermas is working mainly from Marcuse's "Industrialization," see n.30.

4. Translators' Note: The original German version of this essay, *Technik und Wissenschaft als Ideologie*, appeared in a collection which took the same title. See Abbreviations TW.

no room for human self-determination, forming only the infrastructure of the intended realm of freedom (4.3).

Obviously there were problems here that needed to be cleared up. In general outline, it is fair to say that what the Frankfurt critical theorists had in common was their decided antipathy to the secret political aspirations that were being pursued behind the advance of rationalization. But from this common starting point the various thinkers headed off in different directions. Adorno and Horkheimer were more and more keen to discredit *reason itself* in its role as an instrument of domination and oppression (5.1, 8.1). Marcuse, on the other hand, asked us to put our trust in an alternative reason, although, strangely enough, he wanted at the same time to cling to the idea that technology and planned production were political innocents.

Habermas wants to set the house in order. He argues on principle for what Marcuse had grudgingly conceded, namely the acceptability of modern technological achievements. Technico-scientific thinking and activity are one of the basic forms of human existence, *as such* politically neutral but capable of serving humane as well as inhumane ends.[5]

In this connection Habermas turns to the famous theory of Arnold Gehlen. Gehlen claims that technology is no more than an objectified continuation of the purposeful rationality of human labor.[6] What this means is that the functions of the human organism, the tasks of human limbs, human senses, and finally the human brain, have one after the other been transferred to technical devices, starting with the simplest of tools and culminating in the most intricate of computers. If these technical developments follow indeed a logical course that is integrally related to the function of human organs and the structure of physical work, then it is impossible to imagine how we could ever renounce the

---

5. Habermas wants to reinstate the classical Marxist notion of "the political innocence of the forces of production" (TW 58, TRS 89). This has always remained a controversial matter in communism. Note for example communist suspicion of modern cybernetics as commented on by Schuurman, *Technology*, 301–61.

6. Translators' Note: The German *zweckrational*, literally "purpose-rational," is a key term in Habermas (see 6.2 below). Klapwijk is able to translate it fairly directly into Dutch as *doel-rationeel*, but there are a number of possible English equivalents (e.g. "rational goal-directed," TP 169, "purposive-rational," TRS 91). We have generally preferred "goal-rational" or "purposeful rational." As Shapiro points out (TRS vii), the important thing is to understand the term in the sense of "rational with regard to purposes or ends."

progress of modern technology in favor of a technology organized on a totally different basis (TW 56, TRS 87).

If there is such a thing as a dialectic of enlightenment, it can hardly have arisen from the internal logic of technical rationality, since this is just an extension of the human body and human work. Then where does it come from? It is at this point that Habermas introduces a fundamental distinction between work and interaction (TW 62, TRS 91).

Work and Interaction (2)

Habermas takes "work" to mean purposeful rational activity in general, i.e. rational activity aimed at achieving some purpose that is assumed to be fixed under any given circumstances. It is possible to divide this rational activity into "instrumental" and "strategic" activities. Instrumental activity is the rational organization of means to achieve a given purpose, while strategic activity is the rational choice among alternative approaches to the purpose in view. Habermas sometimes includes both of these under "instrumental action" (EI 236, KHI 191). In any case the point here is that the goal-rationality or purposeful rationality of work consists in applying the proper means or determining the proper strategies. Thus it requires both empirical knowledge geared to technical rules, and analytical knowledge geared to the possibilities of choice, with due regard for prevailing values and preferences.

"Interaction," according to Habermas, is totally different from work. "Interaction" refers not to the realization of goals in the field of labor and technology but to the achievement of communication and contact in the sphere of social relationships and practical life. Interaction is not technical or strategic activity but communicative activity making use of the medium of everyday language. Communication also requires knowledge, but knowledge in the sense of mutual understanding. It is geared not to technical rules or strategic models but to socially accepted norms.

Habermas ties this distinction in with the diversity of the sciences. The empirical and analytical sciences represent the systematic continuation of the cumulative learning process that comes along with work and purposeful activity. The historical and hermeneutic (or interpretative) sciences, on the other hand, represent the ordered continuation of the communication processes that operate in the practical interaction of social groups. Since both groups of sciences arise from relationships to certain areas of life, they are bound to them by what Habermas calls an enduring "interest." The empirical and analytical sciences are constantly guided by the "interest" in technical control by means of work. The historical and interpretative sciences are basically determined by the "interest" in mutual understanding by means of language. Since these "knowledge-guiding interests"[7] are basic attitudes towards the world that constitute the meaning and validity of the relevant forms of rationality, Habermas calls them, with appropriate reservations, "transcendental."

Thus there are two sorts of "knowledge-interest," the technical and the practical. But Habermas now distinguishes a third type, which he calls the "emancipatory knowledge-interest." This third orientation arises when human knowledge is critically reflected upon by humans themselves. By inward reflection, knowledge can become transparent to the subject involved. Seen from the perspective of history, humankind comes to its senses, so to speak. That's to say, humans come to understand themselves in work and interaction as ultimately motivated by an interest in maturity and freedom from domination. It is the critically oriented sciences, together with philosophy, that operate on the basis of this attitude and thus reflect on and overturn human knowledge.[8]

Habermas argues that social systems can be distinguished on the basis of the difference between work and interaction and the associated knowledge-interests. In some systems, purposeful rational activity dominates, in others interactional activity is predominant. The institutional framework of society as a whole is bound to be an interactional system, inasmuch as it is formed by norms that give direction to communicative exchange. And there are also certain subsystems, such as those constituted by family and kinship relations, which are typified by norm-guided interaction. Nevertheless, as Habermas sees it, there are other subsystems in which it is not interaction but purposeful rational activity that predominates, for example the economy.

If one compares the great civilizations of the past, it appears that they have time and again been built up around a central political power

---

7. Translators' Note: Habermas speaks of *erkenntnisleitende Interessen* or *Erkenntnisinteressen* (TW 155ff.) Possible English translations include "knowledge-constitutive interests" and "cognitive interests" (KHI 308ff.) as well as "knowledge-interests" (see Shapiro's note on "knowledge," KHI 319).

8. See 7.5 for further comments on the sense in which Habermas labels the cognitive interests "transcendental" (TW 160, EI 240, KHI 311-12, 194-5) and for further reference to the way in which critical reflection can act to liberate (TW 159, EI 244, KHI 310, 197-98).

that is embedded in and "legitimized by" the interactional and communicative relationships of culture and language. More precisely, it is the religious world-views that give their ultimate blessing and sanction to all power and authority within these cultural totalities. Furthermore, it is only within such interactional systems—i.e. within the scope of normative judgments about the meaning and order of the society—that autonomous, purposeful rational subsystems, such as the economy and the production system, are tolerated.

What then do we have to make of the development of modernity that some have called "rationalization" and others the "dialectic of enlightenment"? Habermas's view, expressed in the categories of work and interaction, is as follows. With the advent of bourgeois capitalism, under advancing technology and production, the subsystems of goal-rational activity have gone right out of their bounds. Not only have they put permanent pressure on the interactional relationships of society but they have also completely outdistanced the religious legitimization of the political power.

Capitalism offered a solution to the crisis of authority that it had thus brought about. Instead of legitimizing "from above," it legitimized "from below." Political power was no longer sanctioned in the realm of interaction by divine right and hallowed tradition. Rather power was measured against the new yardstick of what Habermas calls "goal-rationality." And this power was accepted on the interactional level as if it were self-evident, inasmuch as it seemed to be a simple reflection of free-market relationships. It seemed in fact to express the natural "justice" of the principle of economic equivalence, the principle that goods or services that could be exchanged in barter were equivalent in value (TW 69, TRS 97). This bourgeois ideology of liberal capitalism thus seemed to guarantee freedom and neutralize power. The freedom it guaranteed, however, was the freedom of the free market, i.e. of unrestrained entrepreneurial initiative. What actually happened was what Marx's critique of ideology quite rightly exposed, namely that those that were economically stronger took control and were able to do so with the inner conviction that they were acting justly.

Marx and the Snags in Capitalism (3)

History has not stood still since Marx. All sorts of new developments have been afoot since the end of the nineteenth century. Various parts of what Marx called his "critique of political economy" no longer hold good at this latter day stage of capitalism. Habermas turns his attention to four trends in modern capitalism:

(1) increasing intervention by the state,

(2) the more recent legitimization of power,

(3) growing interdependence of science and technology, and

(4) the emergence of a new ideology.

(1) Following in the footsteps of the later Marxists, especially Lenin, Habermas shows how an increasing degree of state intervention has been prompted by a concern to keep the capitalist system on its feet and by a desire to use active economic and socioeconomic policy to crush the crisis phenomena, the class struggle, and the vexatious outgrowths of capitalism. The stability of the economic system has to be secured by actual political interventions. Therefore Marx's view of politics as a "superstructure" that merely reflects socio-economic relationships no longer holds water (TW 75, TRS 101). Politics nowadays is more than just a reflection of the economy.

(2) Marx's critique of the political power system is also superseded, since the ideological foundation of the system, namely the theory of fair exchange or barter, is out of date (TW 76, TRS 102). The modern state looks elsewhere to legitimize its authority. It justifies its interference in social life by appealing to its self-appointed task as guardian and architect of industrial welfare. Technical and economic questions thus do stand at the center of modern politics. The modern welfare state has cooked up a program of substitutes—Habermas calls it an "Ersatzprogrammatik"—a system of compensation, remuneration, and social security. Such measures keep people happy and ensure the loyalty of the masses. Specialists are in control, in politics too, and normative reflection on the practical aims of society, in the sense of free communication and interaction, is banned on the grounds that it endangers the system. The "repoliticization" of the system leads to "depoliticization" of the masses.

(3) Science and technology have become more and more interdependent since the turn of the nineteenth century because of the feedback from technical progress to scientific research. Discoveries are not sporadic any longer but are made by means of co-ordinated research on tasks allocated by the government. Such tasks dominate industrial production,

so much so that they determine its course. Thus Habermas concludes that technology and science have been promoted to the front rank of the production force—they have become an independent source of economic "surplus value." This is why Marx's theory that work is the only source of surplus value has also been superseded (TW 80, TRS 104).

(4) In this way a new ideology appears in the background. Perhaps the best way to describe it is with Karl Jasper's term, as "the superstition of science" ("Wissenschaftsaberglaube")—the superstitious belief that science is the source of welfare and prosperity. As was mentioned earlier, a culture is generally not kept together by technical know-how but by the practice of communication. But modern society deviates from this pattern. It has too much technology and not enough praxis. How is it possible that things have come this far? How is it possible that people put up with it? Habermas maintains that people have swallowed the depoliticization of the masses and pseudo-democratic decision making because of their respect for science. Faith in science deprives the masses of their responsibility and puts them at the mercy of the experts, a technocracy that is only too happy to take over (TW 81, TRS 105). In short, modern capitalism arrives at what we have already been calling "technology and science as ideology." And this ideology can now be interpreted, from the point of view of culture, as the externally imposed and internally accepted overgrowth of technical rationality over practical life, or, from the point of view of human subjects themselves, as the obliteration in human consciousness of the fundamental "dualism" of work and practical interaction (TW 80, 84, 91, TRS 105, 107, 113).

The reason why technocratic ideology is so misleading is that it is not a *pure* projection of impossible happiness, as previous ideologies were. It does in fact give people something they can see and touch, even if it is often a stone instead of bread. Meanwhile the new ideology is hiding the fact that technical and economic progress is no guarantee of practical and moral progress, and does not automatically bring freer communication and more humane relationships (TW 89, TRS 111).

This social critique of Habermas's is aimed not just at Western capitalism but also at bureaucratic socialism in communist countries. The current expectation in Marxist theories is that an increase in productive forces will undermine the established structures and power bases in the modern world. But this just does not hold water in a social order where productive force number one is technical and scientific progress. For this progress is politically managed and serves as justifying principle. In other words, that sort of progress does more to cement established societies than to ferment them.[9]

Dialectic of Enlightenment? (4)

By now it will be clear why Habermas does not adopt Marx's distinction between what are usually called in English "productive forces" ("Produktivkräfte") and "productive relationships" ("Produktionsverhältnisse"). Habermas prefers to replace these categories with the more abstract terms "work" and "interaction." Marx's terminology is simply out of date. The notion of "productive relationships" belongs typically to the period of liberal capitalism in which unrestrained production was indeed allowed to make its mark upon social relationships. But things were not the same before that period, nor have they remained the same since then. The institutionalized relationships in a social order ought to be more generally conceived of as "interaction."

A similar point applies to the term "productive forces." Marx was able in his time to view production as a force, the engine power of social change. Nowadays the production system gives the impression more of a stabilizer than of a driving power in the dynamics of society. Thus the processes of goal-rational activity should also be thought of in more general terms as "work" (TW 92, TRS 113).

To avoid misunderstanding it must be made clear that Habermas is far from regretting the progress of technical-scientific and industrial production in itself. In fact he welcomes the outworking of this progress within all kinds of goal-rational subsystems. Increasing rationalization of work is something he wants to see happening (TW 98, TRS 118–19). The domination of nature by technical reason does not come under attack but is rather applauded.

But it is not only technical reason that Habermas approves of, he also promotes practical-normative reason and the unfettering of interaction in society. The institutional framework of society must move forward,

---

9. TW 88, TRS 110. In practice Marx did make a distinction, according to Habermas, between practical-rational organization of society and technical-scientific domination of nature. But in his thinking about the concept of "social praxis," he reduced communicative activity to instrumental activity. In Habermas's judgment, this is a mechanistic misinterpretation of the so-called dialectic of productive forces and productive relationships—but one that is well entrenched in communist countries (TW 96, 45–46, EI 58, 71, TRS 117, TP 168–9, KHI 42, 52–53). See also 7.3 below.

it cannot keep clinging to relationships that have simply grown on their own and rusted into position. Society too must be rationally controlled and organized. On both levels—technological and social—Habermas, like all Marxists, walks the path of the rationalism of the *Aufklärung*, which wanted to run the world according to rational insight.

What makes Habermas different in this respect is his notion of the fundamental duality of reason. Thus he warns that society ought not to keep reinterpreting and reorganizing itself as a self-regulating mechanism on the model of technical reason (TW 82, TRS 106). This technological self-interpretation is far from self-evident and is actually imposed by political power and ideological violence. But it is a caricature of what authentic interaction should be. Practical deliberation is the very means to detect this caricature. "The structure of symbolic interaction and the role of cultural tradition" are "the only basis on which power and ideology can be comprehended" (EI 58, KHI 42). Thus society must, for its own survival and salvation, reorient itself and measure itself against the norms of practical reason, which open up only in communication that is free of domination (KHI 53, TP 169; "herrschaftsfreie Kommunikation," EI 72, TW 46).

The question may arise whether Habermas's "dialectic of enlightenment" is not just a metaphorical turn of phrase. Isn't he dealing more with the theme of the technological self-interpretation of reason than with the theme of the dialectical reversal of reason?

Habermas certainly puts full emphasis on the danger of an excessive technological self-manifestation of reason. Yet the problem is not just a matter of society being overgrown but of society *letting* itself be overgrown by technology. And this does involve a genuine dialectic. In a way it can even be argued that the dialectical swing of reason counts more heavily and should be taken even more seriously in Habermas than in Horkheimer, Adorno, and Marcuse.

After all, Marcuse ascribed repressive characteristics to reason from the very start (3.2). Back in *Dialectic of Enlightenment*, Horkheimer and Adorno had likewise indicated the bitter connotation of knowledge as such when they quoted Bacon's "knowledge is power" (2.4).[10] Habermas on the other hand takes what is in principle a more positive stand on technical and scientific development. As we saw earlier, he goes so far as to allow that such development might contain an impetus towards the disenchantment and liberation of society.

This makes the dialectical reversal, i.e. the negative outcome of a positive expectation, all the more striking in Habermas. Habermas has to admit that science and technology have themselves cast a new and powerful spell. True enough, the power of the spell has something to do with the successes of science and technology. But it goes beyond that. Society as an institutional whole simply throws itself open to bewitchment and is blinded and paralyzed by it. The spell is strong enough to hold society back from interpreting and justifying itself as an interactional system. *Technology and science as "ideology"*—there you have it: reality remythologized, science made a fetish, the dialectic to a tee.[11]

---

10. Horkheimer had previously had a more positive appreciation of traditional technological science, albeit subject to the critical theory of social activity which he put forward. See the article "Traditional and Critical Theory" in *Critical Theory*, 188–243, and note 3. In his inaugural address "Knowledge and Human Interests," Habermas remarked that he wanted to take up again the thematic distinction that Horkheimer had originally made before him (TW 147, KHI 302).

11. *Technology and science as "ideology"* is the original German title of TW. See also TW 94, 89, TRS 115, 111. Habermas's *theory of science* is thus much more differentiated than that of the later Horkheimer and his colleagues. I do not believe that this allows us to conclude that Habermas is championing a rapprochement between the empirical-analytical and critical-dialectical schools of thought. But the suggestion that it does can be found, for example, in Van Steenbergen, "Jürgen Habermas," 188.

7

Criticism and Liberation in Habermas

THE WAY IN WHICH Habermas views the dialectic of enlightenment determines the way in which he formulates a program of deliverance. If society is shackled by ideology, then the ideology must first and foremost be exposed for what it is. The first thing required then is a critical theory, in the sense of a radical critique of human knowledge.

Habermas's masterly work *Knowledge and Human Interests* presents just such a radical epistemological program, first of all in the spirit of Hegel and secondly following in Marx's footsteps. Ultimately it turns out that a radical epistemology is inevitably "materialist" and coincides with a radical theory of society. The young Habermas too proves to be a Neo-Marxist after all.

Phenomenological Criticism of Knowledge (1)

Habermas's starting point is the decline of the critical tradition since Kant. He considers that Hegel played an ambivalent role in this decline. Hegel did see the circularity, the infinite regression in Kant's criticism. He showed that Kant's critical quest for the structural conditions for human knowledge could be satisfied only by knowledge that in its turn should be open to enquiry about its constitutive conditions, and so on *ad infinitum*. Hegel concluded that Kant had not really followed this epistemology through to the end. If a radically critical epistemology wanted to get anywhere, it would have to reach the ultimate foundation of all knowledge and criticism of knowledge, namely unconditional, absolute knowledge (EI 30, KHI 22-23).

It is not Hegel's radical critique of knowledge that Habermas objects to but the sort of *conclusion* that Hegel's critique leads to. First of all he believes that the only reason why Hegel could arrive at absolute knowledge was because his theory had—uncritically—presupposed precisely that possibility from the outset (EI 18, KHI 12). Moreover he shows, as Adorno did in *Negative Dialectics*, that a radical epistemology that begins to see itself as a force within the overall movement of the absolute, all-embracing mind or spirit, simply runs wild and no longer recognizes any boundaries. A theory of knowledge then converts itself into an identity philosophy that assumes and expounds the absolute unity of subject and object, of mind and matter (5.1). Habermas further notes that an identity philosophy that arrogates the world to itself is ignorant of the vicissitudes of the real history of human consciousness. What really happens, according to Habermas, is that human consciousness develops under the influence of contingent and external impulses and is dependent on the production process among other things (7.3). Habermas has to conclude that Hegel's philosophy is not a genuine theory of knowledge after all and that it does not constitute theoretical and critical reflection on human and scientific knowing. By postulating absolute knowledge, philosophy loses its critical distance from knowledge and science. Identity philosophy simply absorbs all knowing (EI 35, KHI 24).

In Habermas's eyes, Hegel's great merit is on another level. It is to be found not in the outcome of his radicalized theory of knowledge but in its method of working, in phenomenological experience (EI 258, 84, KHI 210, 61–62). A theory of knowledge does not become radical by taking Kant's line that consciousness and its constitutive presuppositions are forms of the general consciousness ("Bewußtsein überhaupt") that are present *a priori,* to be grasped once and for all by a "transcendental deduction." Hegel showed that a theory of knowledge can make itself radical only by seeing and showing that human consciousness and its presuppositions are the result of a cultural and historical evolution.

Habermas refers here to Hegel's *Phenomenology of Spirit*, which gave a critical reconstruction and a fresh systematic account of the entire history of human consciousness. This phenomenological reconstruction is both historical and systematic, since it delineates the whole spiritual history of humankind in a perspective within which this thinking must also situate itself. The phenomenological reconstruction of spiritual development thus leads implicitly to critical reflection on that which most deeply motivates human knowing in its development. And it also leads to an active continuation of it. The insight that sheds light on its own origin and development experiences by this very act a liberating influence. This is the "emancipatory power of reflection" (EI 244, KHI 197).

Thus phenomenology is for Habermas a sort of "maieutic" of the history of the mind, able to deliver history of the hidden truth with which it is pregnant (EI 370, PKHI 159). In Hegel's own philosophy, however, phenomenological experience and illumination unfortunately failed to open history up. What happened instead was that history shut itself tight. And the reason for this, as we saw earlier, was that critical consciousness thought that this was the way to find itself in absolute knowledge, and thus abandoned itself to absolute knowledge (EI 30, KHI 23).

Synthesis through Social Labor and Class Struggle (2)

Whereas Habermas considers Hegel to have elevated and canceled epistemology, he sees Marx as having suppressed and concealed it. Although he realizes that epistemology was suspect in Marx's eyes (EI 43, 85, KHI 30, 62–63), he nevertheless claims that he can see in Marx a man who considered social labor to be not just the basic feature of human being but also the basic character of human knowing. He maintains that Marx's *Theses on Feuerbach* in particular encourage this interpretation.

According to this interpretation, social (or societal) labor is not only an anthropological category but also an epistemological category. Labor in society is not just the basic empirical condition under which humans tackle nature, it is also the basic transcendental condition under which humans apprehend and conceptualize nature (EI 39, KHI 26–27).

For all that, social labor does not have an invariant structure in Marx's thinking. It is not an unchangeable characteristic of the human being. Marx preferred to define humanity from the materialist idea of the unity of nature, such that the human species (as subjective nature) has to come to an "understanding" with the world around (as objective nature). But humans and the world are at the same time set in a historical perspective, since both are involved in a dynamic process of labor that just keeps on developing and by virtue of which humans also just keep on developing.

Viewed in this light, Marx's theory is that there is increasing consciousness at each new level of development in the labor process: There is a continuing synthesis or epistemological connection between the perceiving subject and the material at hand. In this synthesis through social labor ("Synthesis durch gesellschaftliche Arbeit") the human subject—the human species, that is—is supposed to constitute and construct objective reality. Yet at the same time, subject and object will never be identical (as they are supposed to be in Hegel's identity philosophy). This idea that humans by their labor constitute and shape their world suggests a Kantian motif, albeit materialistically interpreted (EI 50, KHI 35–36).

Habermas maintains that we can now discern a further motif in the "synthesis through societal labor" that Marx aimed at. For this synthesis can itself be regarded as a deed or an *action* of the free subject—and, if this is so, the subject does not just constitute its *world* but first of all creates and shapes *itself*. This idea can be found in Fichte (EI 52, KHI 37). So "synthesis through social labor" means that it is in and through labor that humans primarily free themselves and work at their own identity as human beings. In general terms, it becomes possible to talk of human history as the "genesis" or "self-constitution" of the human species, with ceaseless empirical cultural labor going hand in hand with continuous transcendental work on consciousness (EI 41, 43, KHI 29, 31).

Habermas finds this Marxist view of humankind's self-constitution correct enough, but one-sided. He wants to achieve greater clarity than Marx managed. As we have said, Marx discovered and emphasized the way in which humans constitute themselves in labor. But "labor" ought to be understood here as a cumulative process of controlling and comprehending external nature. The history of social labor and production, from this angle, is a linear process, a geometric progression. People are involved in it as a community or as humankind, i.e. as a simple, undivided social subject.[1]

But Marx was also aware of something else. He quite rightly stated that there was a correlate of the process or development of production ("Produktionsprozeß"), namely a "Bildungsprozeß," a formative or educative development in which humankind formed itself not in confrontation with external nature but over against an internal nature, that's to say, a cultural tradition with its own naturally evolved power relationships. Humans reflect on this internal social nature and want to bring it too under rational control. What we have here is a different kind of history, a history of struggle and rivalry, a history of interaction and the self-reflection that goes with it. This "self-formative process" is

---

1. EI 76, KHI 54–55. Just as Marcuse gives his own revised version of Freud (3.4), so Habermas does with Marx—and the new version turns out to be very convenient. Marx actually criticized the idea of the "self-generation of the species" and the notion of an individual, self-created human subject. He dismissed such language as "speculative-idealistic, i.e. fantastic." See "German Ideology," 52.

more of a dialectical than a linear process, dominated as it is by division and potential unification. It is also a process in which a plural human subject—i.e. various social classes—has become involved (EI 81, 83, KHI 58, 60–61).

In Habermas's judgment, Marx did not take sufficient note of the difference between these two processes and as a consequence he interpreted reflection "according to the model of production" (TW 45, EI 61, 85, TP 168, KHI 44, 62). But if there are two different ways in which humans constitute themselves, one via labor and the other via interaction, then we must accept the idea of two kinds of synthesis, the one via social labor in which humans come to an "understanding" with nature, the other via the struggle in society in which the institutionalized classes come to an "understanding" with each other. Synthesis through social labor involves theoretical knowledge; synthesis through class struggle involves practical knowledge. The first is a matter of what Habermas calls "productive knowledge" ("Produktionswissen"); the second is a matter of what he calls "reflective knowledge" ("Reflexionswissen") (EI 77, KHI 56).

The Dialectic of Morality (3)

Modern technology demonstrates just how explosive "productive knowledge" is. To show that "reflective knowledge" is no less explosive, Habermas harks back to idealism again. A third motif now appears in his "materialistic" epistemology, alongside the one from Kant and the one from Fichte. This new element is Hegel's doctrine of the "dialectic of the moral life" or "dialectic of the ethical" (KHI 56; "Dialektik des Sittlichen," EI 77). According to this idea, a disturbance in the moral relationships of a social community, such as a crime, sets off an immanent causal process of rejection or alienation. The punitive justice of "fate" ("Schicksal") turns upon the guilty party. For a crime not only hurts the victim, it also brings suffering on the guilty party. The guilty party has provoked offended society into showing its aversion and exercising its authority; thus the guilty party also suffers, it suffers under society's negative treatment. A social rift opens up. But this negativity experienced on both sides cannot be permanent. Both sides begin to ponder, to feel a longing for what they have lost, to reflect on what has happened, and to see the other side of it. This reflection is what impels humans to strive for recognition and reacceptance. It leads to spontaneous dialog and reconciliation and must eventually restore society as a moral totality.[2]

I have dealt with this appeal to Hegel in some detail, for it beautifully illustrates just why Habermas is so keen on "communication free from domination" in a world of power and negativity. Now Habermas states that Marx did not give sufficient recognition to this emancipatory force of reflection in society. Marx did not completely ignore the Hegelian dialectic of morality, but he did draw a distorted picture of it, since he interpreted it in terms of the dialectic of class antagonism, a dialectic that was meant to be directly related to the level of production and organization of labor. According to Marx, rationalization of labor leads to a slackening of the need for social oppression, even though it may not mean an immediate reduction in the oppression itself. It would mean that the illegitimacy of institutionalized oppression will become more and more obvious. The difference between the oppression that actually exists and the oppression that is still justifiable would give an objective measure of the extent to which the moral balance is disturbed (using Hegelian terms) or a measure of the amount of surplus repression (using Marcuse's terms, as explained in 3.4). This visible difference would set in motion the causal mechanism of "fate," provoke revolution, and eventually bring the warring parties together. But only temporarily—as long as economic scarcity has not been totally eliminated, further domination will be necessary and new class war will be stirred up, until perfected production finally banishes scarcity and brings the dialectic to its rest (EI 80, KHI 58–59).

This interpretation of Hegel's moral dialectic is too mechanistic for Habermas's liking. Marx has directly related the social dialectic and the possibility of ending it to the need to combat scarcity and to the level of production.[3] But the way things have gone in the modern industrialized countries is for Habermas, as it was for Marcuse, glaring proof that welfare in itself is no guarantee of justice or morality. "Liberation from

---

2. TW 46, EI 78, TP 169, KHI 56. Habermas considers that reflection and blindness can co-exist. "In the act of solitary self-reflection the subject can deceive itself." Thus *Aufklärung* can succeed only to the extent that the parties on *both* sides are suffering and searching for enlightenment. See *Theorie und Praxis*, 34, TP 28.

3. We can join Van der Hoeven in putting it even more strongly: As Marx began to put more emphasis on practical revolutionary action, so he wanted to give this *negative* practice a sturdier motivation by appealing to the *positivistic* basis of production, *Marxisme en Revolutie*, 31.

hunger and misery does not necessarily converge with liberation from servitude and degradation" (TW 46, TP 169). Unlike Hegel, Marx did not see that the moral dialectic and the war between classes that are offended have their own interactional status as a "movement" of reflection (EI 81, KHI 58). Marx was too much dazzled by the factor of production that loomed so large in the nineteenth century.[4]

The point is, however, that the production process develops only in an objective connection with the social self-formative process (EI 83, TW 47, KHI 60, TP 169). Or, as Habermas puts it, the "Produktionprozeß" and the "Bildungsprozeß" are "interdependent" (EI 77, KHI 55). The process of production develops along with the history of the social classes, a history that is propelled by reflection. In short, the history of production is embedded in the framework of total social praxis and cannot be correctly described except in that setting.

The division of labor and the organization of production certainly do have an objective effect on relations of ownership and the class struggle within the history of the society. To that extent the dialectic of the class struggle is indeed provoked and mediated by the production process (EI 84, KHI 62). But we must not miss the broader social context. When we take the wider view we see how the dialectic of the class struggle has been institutionalized in gnarled traditions, severed moral relationships, distorted language, and curtailed communication. And this cracked and warped society is usually painted over with a layer of ideological varnish. Ideology is the very force that—deceptively but effectively—restricts communication, puts a legal stamp on the prevailing relationships of labor and authority, and gives society its outward appearance. Ideology blocks the self-formative process of humankind.

Thus development of the forces of production is in itself not capable of breaking the spell of ideology. What it can do is to heighten the disproportionate contrast between necessary repression and the repression that is actually imposed in society. In this way, albeit indirectly, it can sharpen people's vague awareness of the dislocation of moral relationships. But according to Habermas, none of this alters the fact that this

---

4. Despite the present obvious dangers of unrestricted growth, this is precisely what Marxism in communist countries continues to set its heart on as the hope for the future. "The development of the productive forces provides again and again the main impetus to the progress of productive relationships and to revolutionary changes in them," De Leeuwe, *Marxisme*, 62. Harmsen offers some evidence of second thoughts on this issue in his *Natuur*, esp. 44, 49.

awakening is a matter of critical reflection at the level of interrupted communication itself. It is even possible here to make a case that when Marx unmasked the "objective illusion" of commodity fetishism, i.e. the ideology of nineteenth century capitalism, he did so not by presenting facts about production but by critique of ideology (EI 82, KHI 59–60).

Theory Equals Therapy (4)

We have begun to see how Habermas pulls the threads of his argument together. He shares with his colleagues of the Frankfurt School the conviction that society is caught in a web of myth and ideology that can be torn apart only by theoretical and critical reflection. Now we can detect what Habermas takes "critical reflection" to mean and how he works both Hegel's epistemology and Marx's sociology into his own account of the dialectic of reflection.

The dialectic of reflection is in the first instance phenomenological in the Hegelian sense: Consciousness, reflecting on the problem of knowledge, recalls the progress of humankind's consciousness. Moreover, it illuminates this historical phenomenon not only *from* a critical standpoint but also, by reconsidering the present in the light of the past, in order to *arrive at* a more advanced critical standpoint.

Habermas has, however, transplanted this phenomenology of emerging consciousness, which is the heart of Hegel's *Phenomenology of Spirit*, into a Marxist theory of society. The drift of this is first and foremost that the reflecting subject cannot be equated with a unitary human-divine spirit, but consists in a plurality of social classes. It is therefore impossible to speak of a universal history of the mind, only of particular developments of consciousness, articulated in class relationships. Furthermore, in the phenomenological reconstruction of human consciousness, even the reconstruction itself shares in life's fragmentation. So it cannot be effected from an absolute position (as Hegel would have it), only from a "phenomenologically mediated mode of thought" (EI 85, KHI 62).[5] Nevertheless, this "epistemological refraction of the light of phenomenological self-reflection," this class perspective, is not the last word. For class-consciousness that manages to focus on itself and

---

5. Translators' Note: Habermas's German wording is *phenomenologisch gebrochene Einstellung*, literally "phenomenologically broken attitude." Habermas perhaps alludes to the "breaking" of the light of phenomenological knowledge, and the word "refracted" may therefore be more appropriate.

to see itself in phenomenological perspective for what it is, does come to its senses and does free itself from its own one-sidedness, surpassing its own class-consciousness. In this way it breaks through the objective illusion and the ideological necessity of the class antagonism to which it was previously subjected (EI 85, KHI 61–62).

The only problem is this: Why should class-consciousness manage this critical self-reflection and thereby escape from ideological delusion? Here we reach what may well be the ultimate truth in Habermas's eyes. It is what Hegel called the dialectic of morality. Habermas finds here his conviction that "fate" will sooner or later come into operation in a disturbed or fragmented society. Here is the dialectical mechanism of critical self-reflection, recognition of one's isolation, and reacceptance of one's abandoned opponent. The rift drives us to reflect, and reflecting drives us to break through the ideologically entangled class antagonism—it drives us to reconciliation.

As we have already seen, the view of the Frankfurt School is that the dialectic of enlightenment has drawn modern society under the spell of a new myth or ideology. The only way out—and this now proves to be Habermas's view as well—is to ride the wave of the dialectic and thus eventually to reach renewed *Aufklärung* (EI 373, PKHI 161). All that is required is an epistemology or critique of knowledge that is radical. And an epistemology can be radical only if it can diagnose itself as a theory of society (EI 59, 372, KHI 42, PKHI 160). As phenomenology, it must not present the glorious march of absolute knowledge but the painful gait of a disheveled and disfigured society, the institutionalized product of interactional interruptions, communicative short-circuiting, and ideological violence.

Despite all the planners and technocrats, technological breakthroughs do not bring direct benefits to modern society. Society would be far better off if there were a breakthrough in ideologically imprisoned communication. Here too a renewed enlightenment is necessary, an en-light-enment. This enlightenment dawns where a critique of knowledge radicalizes itself into a critique of society and ideology (EI 85, KHI 63). In so doing, it dispels blindness and allows opinion to be formed openly and without manipulation.

The light of this critique of knowledge is by nature beneficial. It enables the social classes to see themselves as they really are, suffering at each other's hands in short-circuited communication and distorted perspective. By the very act of showing that the distorted picture is indeed distorted, critical insight eliminates the distortion. Critical insight is liberation, and not just liberation purely within the mind. It is a liberation that leads from social criticism to social change. Indeed, it overturns social relationships and the cultural self-formative process (EI 372, PKHI 160).

In other words, the theory itself amounts to a therapy (EI 348, KHI 287). Habermas's favorite illustration of this is Freudian psychology. In essence, what happens in psychoanalysis is that a "process of enlightenment" is initiated and the patient is driven to "self-reflection" (EI 299, KHI 235). The patient has to call to mind the repressed conflicts of the past that have previously been coming to expression only in disturbed communication and divorced symbolism, in misconceptions and obsessions. By this means the patient can be freed from repression (EI 262, KHI 215). Thus in psychoanalysis too, the reflection and liberation that one aims for are virtually an interaction that takes place in communication between patient and physician.[6]

Emancipatory Interest (5)

Although Habermas is struck by the dialectic of enlightening and blinding, he doggedly persists in viewing world history as humankind's process of development from nature to freedom. In this process of emancipation, as we saw earlier, humans constitute themselves in the cultural patterns of labor and language, and thus also constitute themselves in the technical and practical knowing that result from these patterns.

Since the technical knowledge-interest makes the exact sciences possible, while the practical knowledge-interest makes the historical sciences possible, these interests, being objective preconditions of science, might be called "transcendental." But they are transcendental only in a limited sense, for they are certainly not invariant, supratemporal structures of the mind. These "knowledge-guiding interests" have arisen out of the life-relationships of work and interaction, and ultimately out of the human being's own emergence from nature. From *nature* or *from*

---

6. EI 290, KHI 232. In this connection Habermas dissociates himself, more explicitly than Marcuse did, from Freud's scientism (as commented on in 3.3). I am referring to Freud's attempts to look back on psychoanalytical treatment and reinterpret it in terms of the natural sciences, as if it could be compared with biochemical intervention, EI 301, 309, 346, KHI 239, 246, 205.

nature? If we stress "nature," then the knowledge-interests seem to have a contingent, natural origin. Then they are little more than particular empirical urges of *Homo sapiens* to preserve itself. If we stress "from," however, then the interests seem to be more than accidental, more than something that "just happened." Then knowledge does still contain a natural urge to self-preservation, but the urge is broken and transcended. Then the knowledge interests do have something like a transcendental status. With respect to science they are, in Habermas's turn of phrase, "quasi-transcendental systems of reference."[7]

The same must be said, *mutatis mutandis*, about the emancipatory knowledge-interest. After rising up out of nature (as in Marx's materialist vision), humans have, by virtue of reflecting phenomenologically on themselves and on the dialectic of their development, freed themselves from the compulsion and command of nature. Knowledge on its way towards radical self-knowledge converges with the emancipatory interest (as in Hegel's idealistic vision). "In self-reflection, knowledge for the sake of knowledge comes to coincide with the interest in autonomy and responsibility (*Mündigkeit*). For the pursuit of reflection knows itself as a movement of emancipation" (EI 244, TW 164, KHI 197–98, 314).

There is a sort of interplay between the technical and practical interest in knowledge and the emancipatory interest in knowledge. Looking at it materialistically, we have to say that the emancipatory interest cannot develop except in and through a communication system that has been distorted by force. Thus the emancipatory interest depends on the technical and practical interests and their concrete forms of development. Looking at it critically and reflectively, however, we are bound to say that the technical and practical interests are not seen to be transcendental, their misshapenness is not revealed, until they are brought in relation to the interest in maturity. Revolution must be linked with reflection on repression.[8]

A criticism that has been made of Habermas both by Theunissen from a Catholic standpoint and by Rohrmoser from a Protestant stand-

7. KHI 194–5 ("quasi-transzendentale Bezugssysteme," EI 240). For further comments on the transcendental yet empirical status of the knowledge-guiding interests, see EI 350, TW 162, KHI 288–89, 313, also TP 7, 14, 21ff.

8. For the dependence of the emancipatory interest on technics, praxis and power, see EI 259, 290, KHI 212, 232–33, and also EI 400, PKHI 176 and TP 22. For the recognition of interests as transcendental (interests in which reason is inherent, EI 349, KHI 287) on the basis of the interest in maturity, see EI 244, KHI 197–198.

point is that Habermas's emancipatory interest is really only subjective, factual, and natural. According to them it is not transcendental at all, since it is grounded in a subject given in nature, namely the empirically accidental fact of the human species. If it is true, they argue, that the only things innate in humanity are humanity's natural interests, then a theory of emancipation makes itself impossible or, at the very least, superfluous. If humans have only natural interests, then, according to Rohrmoser, the sober observation would suffice that today's society evidently has a natural interest in remaining the way it is.[9]

In my opinion, Habermas is credited here with a conclusion that he himself would not accept. He explains the emancipating power of reason and the transcendental status of the quest for maturity not on the basis of humankind as an empirical subject but on the basis of the dialectical history of human self-constitution. In this history the human species transcends itself. Being on the move, humans struggle by means of self-reflection and recollection to become more than just natural beings with natural needs and concerns. It is in this way that humanity gets to know itself and to discern its own emancipatory interest.

But Habermas has to face two questions here. The first is how the emancipation process could ever have got going, since humankind was by origin nothing but a natural being set in a material nature. "A part of nature acquires, through us, autonomy in nature," he says (KHI 311; "Ein Stück Natur erwirbt sich durch uns Autonomie in der Natur," TW 160). But how is this conceivable? Can Marxist materialism justifiably appeal to Kant's "fact of reason" as if it were a "fact of nature"? (EI 417, 416, PKHI 185) Isn't nature being asked to support what nature cannot support?

The second question is how the emancipation process can continue nowadays in a society that has been institutionally warped by anonymous power and ideological violence. The road that Habermas directs us down seems not so much one of reconciliation with nature as one of reconciliation in moral and social relationships by means of com-

---

9. See Theunissen, *Gesellschaft*, 24f., 30f., and Rohrmoser, *Elend der kritischen Theorie*, 102ff. Compare Habermas's reply in EI 415f. (PKHI 184f.). Rohrmoser and Theunissen stress the objectivity of human striving for maturity and accuse Habermas of ignoring it. But the idea of this objectivity, pointing to the ontological-metaphysical status of history or to some "absolute" in history, seems to rest more on Hegelian metaphysics than on Christian faith. For my own comments on the difference between these two ideas, see Klapwijk, "Geloof en rede," 77ff.

munication without domination ("herrschaftsfreie Kommunikation").[10] But he himself is forced to recognize that a manipulated world adopts a posture of resistance against such rational communication (TW 99, TRS 119–20). Isn't this another vicious circle, much as we found in Marcuse and Adorno? Freedom presupposes rational dialog, but rational dialog presupposes freedom.[11]

In modern society freedom is non-existent, and institutionalized dialog is impracticable. The "domination system" prefers to gloss over social oppositions and class warfare rather than bring them out into the open (TW 86, TRS 109). As a result of all this, what is endangered is not a particular class interest but the emancipatory interest of humankind itself. History stagnates. The dialectic of liberation has come to a halt. "The suspended dialectic of the ethical generates the peculiar semblance of post-histoire" (TW 88, TRS 110).

How then is communication, distorted by power, to be brought to life? Where is the repressed conflict of an unreconciled society to come out into the open? Habermas's answer lies in the area of public opinion, in processes of democratic decision-making, in an open pragmatic debate among scientists, academics, and politicians. For it is especially in this area that bondage predominates and that the depoliticization and manipulation of the masses have gone farthest. Thanks to the so-called mass communication media!

Who is to get the campaign rolling? To begin with, Habermas looked among students and pupils for "the only protest potential" (TW 100, TRS 120). Subsequently he became more and more critical and distrustful, until finally at a 1967 student conference in Hamburg he wrote student agitation off as "left-wing fascism." He was actually backed up by Horkheimer, who was at that time warning students that for all their high-minded intentions they could end up playing into the hands of left-

---

10. Habermas, "Ein philosophierender Intellektueller," 42. Habermas here expresses his reservations about the syntheses with nature which Horkheimer and Adorno are looking for.

11. "A reasonable dialog between reasonable men must presume their autonomy, if there is to be a opening up of the communication that has been ideologically constrained and distorted by dominant interests" ("Ein vernünftiger Dialog von Vernünftigen muß deren Autonomie immer schon voraussetzen, wenn die ideologisch eingeschränkten und durch Herrschaftsinteressen verzerrte Kommunikation aufgebrochen werden soll," Rohrmoser, "Autonomie," 157. For remarks on the problem of circularity in Marcuse and Adorno, see 4.4, 5.2, and 9.3.

wing state bureaucracies whose totalitarian practices were suspiciously like right-wing reigns of terror.[12]

In all of this Habermas was searching for a way in which theory and practice could be combined. He wanted a flexible strategy that could move between the enlightenment of reflection and the political struggle that had to be coupled to it. At the same time it has to be said that he began to have more and more serious doubts about the feasibility of a renewed *Aufklärung* or of an opening up of public opinion or of an about-turn in public relationships[13]

Again we have come back to the dialectic of enlightenment. It is all very well for Kant to have talked in the context of enlightenment about reason's being a "fact" ("das Faktum der Vernuft") but is it still possible to talk about such a "fact" in the face of a dialectic of enlightenment such as even Habermas recognizes? If a freedom that has been so painstakingly won over the centuries can be so quickly lost, then isn't the great fact of life the fact of *un*reason? Habermas would not agree—but what then is his underlying motivation? In Horkheimer's later writings the fact of *un*reason does indeed loom up like a dark cloud that cannot be dispelled.

---

12. See Van Steenbergen, "Jürgen Habermas," 178, and Horkheimer, *Critical Theory*, viii.

13. Compare Habermas, *Strukturwandel der Öffentlichkeit*, 211ff, "The Scientization of Politics and Public Opinion" (TW 138f., 144, TRS 75f., 79) and "Some Difficulties in the Attempt to Link Theory and Practice" (TP 3ff.). See also Van Houten, *Tussen aanpassing en kritiek*, 281.

8

Horkheimer and Religious Yearning

THIS BOOK BEGAN WITH a reference to the republication of *Dialektik der Aufklärung* in 1969. In the preface that accompanied that second edition, Horkheimer and Adorno declared that the dialectical reversal from enlightenment into mythical worship of positive facts had firmly established itself in the postwar period. Horkheimer has expressed himself in similar terms on other occasions. For example, the conclusion to his address entitled "Threats to Freedom" at the Twelfth Protestant Church Conference (Evangelische Kirchentag) in Germany in 1965 was that the notion of individual freedom no longer had any meaning whatsoever in countries like Communist China. But even in the Western world, he said, individual freedom was threatened with extinction by the positivistic mentality of an enlightenment that had swung around into its very opposite ("die in ihr Gegenteil umgeschlagene Aufklärung," KV 353, CR 158).

The Immanent Logic of History (1)

Horkheimer's philosophical testament is his much read *Die Sehnsucht nach dem ganz Anderen* (The Yearning for the Totally Other). Originally an interview in *Der Spiegel* in January 1970, it was later revised and published in book form. The most harrowing point in the interview is when Horkheimer, answering a pointed question, virtually concedes that the course of history, the dialectic of enlightenment, is no longer reversible: "The immanent logic of history, as I understand it at the moment, does in fact lead to the administrated world ('die verwaltete Welt')." "I assume that the process cannot be undone, except by horrifying disasters such as nuclear war." And he says elsewhere that the advance towards this automated world domination will grind and shudder along as the great power blocs engage in a terrifying conflict and as what little remains of individual human freedom, especially in the West, is liquidated.[1]

Adorno spoke of the need for *reason* to hibernate in the faint hope that the winter might one day end, but Horkheimer thinks a new spring is not just improbable but impossible. Historical developments have already gone too far. Humans *must* take control of nature. The explosion of technology, population growth, competition among the great powers—such things make global administration inescapable. Tremendous natural forces, like nuclear energy, have been unleashed, and only some central controlling agency will be able to restrain them (SA 83–84).

The other side of the coin is that individuality is being whittled away. The individual becomes a replaceable spare part, and freedom gives way to instinctive behavior. Free will? The world of humans will begin to look like a beehive or an anthill, teeming with activity to be sure, yet infinitely tedious. Perhaps innocuous drugs will have to be used to alleviate the boredom, but boredom there will certainly be, for life will no longer have any meaning (SA 84, 88).

Religion Unveils Finiteness and Injustice (2)

When Horkheimer is asked what the meaning of life depends on, his firm answer is "God." "Without God one will try in vain to preserve absolute meaning" (KV 227, CR 47, SA 69).

This assertion is wide open to misunderstanding. Horkheimer surely does not mean to say that he believes in God. He regards faith as a Protestant invention (SA 59). Nor does Horkheimer want to claim that we could have knowledge of God other than through faith, let alone that we could prove God's existence. Even to use the word "God" is really going too far for Horkheimer. He would rather stick with terms like "the absolute" or "the totally other." For we can say nothing about God. God cannot be named and no idea or image can be formed (SA 56–57, 77).

This is reminiscent of Adorno's metaphysics of the absolute (5.5). Both Horkheimer and Adorno not only look at the idea of God's unknowability in relation to the Judeo-Christian taboo on images of God, but also describe it as a crucial axiom of the critical theory in itself (SA 57). Horkheimer follows Adorno in presenting this basic orientation to

---

1. SA 83, 82 and the preface to *Kritische Theorie* (vol. 1, xi).

the unknowable absolute as "yearning" ("Sehnsucht"). It is a nostalgia, a longing, but no more than that.²

Neo-Marxist scholars, including some outside the Frankfurt School, commonly relate religion to the search for life's meaning.³ Time and again they capture religion in categories like yearning and hope. They do not understand it as a trusting faith, founded on divine revelation and expressible in tenets or doctrines. So if we find people such as Horkheimer talking about the connection between religious yearning and the search for meaning, then we must realize that they are talking in terms of the meaning that human subjects give to the world, not the meaning that God confers. In fact in 1935 Horkheimer had already said that religion embodied the desires and longings, the complaints and accusations of countless generations.⁴

Religion offers meaning because it forms the precondition for human awareness of finiteness (SA 57, 71) and of injustice (SA 68). First of all religion keeps alive the notion of human finiteness. Marx awakened the proletariat to their distress and oppression with a view to social revolution, but their solidarity was short-lived and their lot was improved without revolution. There is another distress, however, that permanently unites all people and that springs from their material and mortal nature, from their forlornness and suffering. Only religion, the thought of something totally other, something totally different and infinite, can bring home to overconfident humans the distress of their finiteness and

---

2. Adorno tried to clarify this yearning by looking at the limited nature of concepts, while Horkheimer follows Kant and Schopenhauer in working from the relative nature of the world. The world that presents itself to us is a world of phenomena that are relative, stirring us to think of something other, something absolute in the background (SA 61, 75, KV 211). The difference between Kant and Schopenhauer is that the latter did not posit the definite existence of God on the basis of this "other" (KV 256, 259, CR 73–74, 76).

3. I am thinking here of writers such as Machovec, *Vom Sinn*; Garaudy, *L'Homme Chrétien*, esp. 28; Kolakowski, *Mensch ohne Alternative*, esp. 279; English translation: *Marxism and Beyond*, 58, 22ff., and Bloch, *Prinzip Hoffnung*, esp. 1404.

4. See "Thoughts on Religion" in *Critical Theory*, 129–31. Horkheimer says here: ". . . just as reason after [*sc.* according to] Kant, even though it knows better, cannot avoid falling into shattered but nonetheless recurring illusions, so too, ever since the transition from religious longing to conscious social practice, there continues to exist an illusion which can be exposed but not entirely banished. It is the image of a perfect justice." *Critical Theory*, 129; also taken up in SA 67).

give them solidarity in the struggle for a world in which there is more living and less suffering. Only religion rescues humanity for humans.

Religion also keeps alive the notion of human injustice. Horkheimer recalls a passage in one of Victor Hugo's works: "An old woman is walking along the street, she has brought up her children and got little thanks for it, she has toiled hard and lives in misery, she has loved and is left on her own. Yet she is far from hating, and helps wherever she can. Someone sees her going on her way and says 'Ça doit avoir un lendemain,' 'there has to be a tomorrow'" (KV 212). Hugo's idea matches that fundamental conviction of Kant, the philosopher of the enlightenment: injustice cannot be final. Horkheimer's terse way of saying it is "Religion is the yearning that the murderer will not triumph over the innocent victim" (SA 62).

In other words, religion equals a hunger for complete justice (SA 69). It may be atheistic religion in a right-wing dictatorship or theistic religion in a left-wing bureaucracy.[5] But without religion, in whatever shape or form, morality fades away. For the difference between good and evil is not rationally explicable or scientifically deducible (SA 60). Thus rational deliberation about norms in society, such as we find in Habermas, does not really carry any weight so far as Horkheimer is concerned. "All ethics ultimately goes back to theology" (SA 61). Without any notion of God, there is no notion of eternal truth (KV 227, CR 48). Without any reference to the transcendent, moral matters become matters of arbitrary taste (KV 236). Without theology, politics is just so much business, however sophisticated (SA 60). Only religion rescues the possibility of morals and ethics (SA 69).

With this concept of religion, Horkheimer stands in opposition to the modern theologians. He is opposed to his former Frankfurt colleague Paul Tillich with his symbolic interpretation of God as "the ground of being," opposed to Bishop John Robinson and his abstract clichés, opposed to all the American "God-is-dead" theologians. In Horkheimer's eyes, modern theology has been infected by positivistic thinking and as a result makes unnecessary compromises with science, a fruitless exercise anyway since positivism has nothing to say to theology (KV 233, 350).

But Horkheimer is equally opposed to the more conservative theologians with their doctrines of God's omnipresence, omnipotence, and

---

5. In this conception of religion the traditional distinction between theism and atheism becomes irrelevant (KV 228, CR 49).

providence. So far as Horkheimer is concerned, when the best is spoiled it is worst of all. For the doctrine of God's omnipresence removes the human feeling of loneliness, while the doctrines of God's omnipotence and providence and the resurrection of the dead trivialize suffering and thus remove the human sense of injustice.[6]

Between Longing and Fear (3)

What value is there in these religious pronouncements of Horkheimer's later life? We should bear in mind that *Die Sehnsucht nach dem ganz Anderen* does not mark the belated conversion of a Marxist, nor is it, as someone has suggested, "the deathbed confession of a heretic" (SA 5). Horkheimer's idea of God can be found in embryo right back in his 1935 paper "Thoughts on Religion."[7] After all, as we saw earlier, he considered religious yearning to be of general relevance to the critical theory. When all is said and done, Horkheimer is not so different from Marx, who for his part similarly characterized religion as "the expression of real suffering as well as the protest against real suffering." The difference is that Marx went further and claimed that religion was a fit of intoxication to make the misery acceptable—hence religion was "the opium of the people."[8] Horkheimer would prefer to draw some finer distinctions here. He would prefer to make a distinction between the historically determined suffering of a social class and the universal distress of humankind. And so far as this universal existential distress is concerned, he wants to say that the religious expression of it is indispensable, and that it is only the dogmatic fixation of it that is intoxicating.

The emphasis on religious nostalgia in Horkheimer's later work is nonetheless striking. This "homesickness" is undoubtedly related to

---

6. SA 56–57, 77. See Horkheimer's letter to the Fischer publishing company, *Kritische Theorie*, vol. 2, xi, KV 247, CR 61–62. (Horkheimer's letter is not included among the translations in *Critical Theory*.) Horkheimer's criticism is an alarming misrepresentation of the biblical revelation concerning God's judgment on sin and injustice. Horkheimer's rationalist perspective blurs this aspect of revelation, which ought to be taken just as seriously as the message of God's saving power.

7. Reprinted in *Critical Theory*, 129–31. Furthermore there are at least four places where the editor, H. Gumnior, has taken sections from the 1935 essay and incorporated them into SA (54, 67, 68–69 and 69). Horkheimer has thus reaffirmed these statements some thirty-five years later.

8. Marx, "Towards the Critique of Hegel," 250.

Horkheimer's dialectic of enlightenment and the idea that the world has become anything but humanity's "home."

Thus the logic of history, this immanent and inevitable development of culture that we referred to earlier, is certainly tied up with religious yearning. This logic of history arouses nostalgia—and also eats the heart out of it. How can religion express and allay people's deepest distress when people are being sealed up inside a beehive? "The more progress, the greater the threat to freedom," says Horkheimer. Or "I have come more and more to the view that one should talk not so much of religious yearning but of the fear that this God is not there" (SA 75–76). The automated future is at hand. Then everything theological will be done away with. The search for meaning will be abandoned and serious philosophy will be treated as childish crotchetiness (SA 88).

The Critical Theory Compromised (4)

Adorno's *Negative Dialectics* still talks of "yearning" as longing for a reconciled nature, for an almost inconceivable utopia where bodiliness and spirit are unified (5.5). At the end of the famous interview in *Der Spiegel*, it emerges that Horkheimer finds this utopian world not only impracticable but even impossible in principle. The "totally other" falls to pieces, history disintegrates, enlightened reason seems to be a will-o'-the-wisp, and the realm of reconciliation and freedom yields to descending darkness.

In a 1962 paper, "Kants Philosophie und die Aufklärung," Horkheimer was still straightforwardly advocating the realm of freedom as the unity of freedom and justice, the ideal of the *Aufklärung* and the heart of Kant's philosophy (KV 215). Now this high ideal has split into two warring notions: "The more justice, the less freedom; the more freedom, the less justice." In other words, freedom and justice are "dialectical concepts" (SA 86). Justice must be rationally organized and will therefore destroy individual freedom and human self-development.

The dialectic of enlightenment? Perhaps even at the very start enlightenment was already turned against itself. Perhaps the joyful slogan "liberty, equality, and fraternity" was a dismal paradox (SA 86). The realm of freedom, which Marx too dreamed of, is not coming into view. Indeed it cannot come into view, and for three reasons. First, because modern society is headed for automation, not liberty. Secondly, because freedom and justice are incompatible. And thirdly, because free self-development presupposes scarcity and distress, and because a streamlined world stifles the slightest mental effort.[9] What is left over of that longing for a completely different world? Totalitarianism and anarchism loom up as the two hideous alternatives. Or do we perhaps have to listen to Schopenhauer and does the ego have to perpetuate itself by abdication and surrender to nature?[10]

Still, there is hardly any sense in weighing up the alternatives. The only genuine alternative is the inevitable approach of the totalitarian world. All that remains for the critical theory is to weigh the pros and cons of the present and the future. The theory tells us how much the new order will cost, that's all. As we said before, organized justice costs you your liberty (SA 76). The price you have to pay for the pill is the death of erotic love (SA 74). To pay for the emancipation of modern self-assured woman we have to sacrifice the love and warmth that mothers used to have (SA 80–81). To pay for the father's mythical authority to be dismantled we have to sell moral conscience, and so on (SA 80). At least you know what's coming.

When Horkheimer is finally asked what use there is in such criticism of society and whether we can prevent the rise of the "administrated world," his answer is tragic: "No, we can't. But we can perhaps help to steer the course of events away from periods or horrors and atrocities." "To give voice to what one knows and thereby perhaps to avert new terror remain the right of a man who is really still alive."[11] In other words, the critical theory must try to make the painful transition to the automated world as bearable as possible. What can be said of this? You can take it as a final sympathetic declaration of solidarity with violated humankind. But if you listen carefully, you can also catch a note of complicity in the dialectic of enlightenment, the strains of actual involvement in the termination of human freedom.

---

9. Horkheimer, *Verwaltete Welt?* 30, 20–21.
10. Habermas, "Ein philosophierender Intellektueller," 42.
11. SA 87 and *Critical Theory*, viii.

9

The Myth and the Messianic Light

IT IS NOW MANY years since the Frankfurt School ceased to form a solid body of scholars at the University of Frankfurt. Adorno died in 1969, Horkheimer in 1973 (when he was already retired), and Habermas became director of the Max Planck Institute in Starnberg in 1971. Their critical theory nevertheless continues to have an amazing influence. After Adorno's death, Marcuse rightly remarked that "the debate with Adorno has yet to begin." Meanwhile the publishers Suhrkamp Verlag are in the process of publishing Adorno's complete works in twenty volumes. The works of other Frankfurt scholars also keep being reprinted and republished. Habermas continues to write prolifically, while there are many other thinkers pursuing a similar line, such as Karl-Otto Apel, Alfred Schmidt, Albrecht Wellmer, Rolf Tiedemann and Axel Honneth. Given that there is a general renaissance in the study of critical theory and that there are social problems on a global scale, we can assume that the real debate with the Frankfurt School is indeed yet to begin.

A World Turned Harsh (1)

The Frankfurt scholars' critical theory is first of all a razor-edged critique of Western society. I agree with Rohrmoser that their criticism has dug right under the foundations of those basic democratic structures of the so-called free world that were always taken for granted.[1] Stripping away the ideological veneer compels society to think again about the aims of education, about the bases of law and the state, about the management of technology and the economy, indeed about the fundamental direc-

---

1. Rohrmoser, "Problematiek van de rede," 87.

tion that Western culture and society have long been taking and that has proved to be more and more aggressive and imperious.

The Frankfurt scholars' criticism is directed not only against the Western world. It also includes a fierce indictment of left-wing state bureaucracies and collectivist systems in Eastern Europe or anywhere else where they occur, from Cuba to China. What is surprising about Neo-Marxist criticism in this connection is the claim—and it is a criticism I find it hard to get away from—that capitalism and left-wing systems are close relatives, offspring of the same stock. They may be adversaries on the economic plane, but as conceptions of society and culture they are both inspired by one and the same principle, the "principle of domination."

Many people may find this a painful observation. If true, it means that criticism of the totalitarian characteristics of communism and its contemporary leftist derivates is not authentic unless it also slices into Western imperialism. And the reverse also applies: Criticism of the capitalist plunder of the Third World, for instance, is not credible unless it also takes account of the exploitation of humankind in Soviet-style states or other autocratic regimes. Of course, in this perspective a post-communist combination of the two systems, such as capitalism under socialist management or whatever one might like to call it, may well be a nice mixture, but *at heart* it will not be one scrap better.

The newspapers bring us cynical news from different continents. Thousands of young seals are killed by being battered to death so that their skins will not be damaged. This in the name of free commerce. On the Killing Fields of Cambodia hundreds of young people are battered to death in order to save bullets. This in the name of a liberating revolution. With freedom on everyone's lips, a wave of violence engulfs all that lives and moves. Who even notices? Who collects the countless tears, as it says in Psalm 56? The sole advantage of the bruised and battered citizens of the Third World must surely be that they feel the most pain and therefore see more clearly than anyone else that the blows they suffer, whether from left or right, East or West, speak of domination.

The world has turned harsh. With an amazing ease and naturalness, human life has been objectified, "thing-ified." In Western countries abortion is a thousand times easier than adoption. Aren't the Frankfurt theorists right? Isn't the principle of domination the real motive by which modern humans actually live, while they piously swear by a different principle, the motive of maturity and freedom? Hasn't freedom indeed swung around into dictatorship? Isn't the dialectic of enlightenment a massive reality?

The Dialectic and its Many Meanings (2)

"Dialectic of enlightenment"—that is the formula in which Horkheimer, Adorno, and their colleagues have captured the secrets of our world and our age. The well-known dictionary of philosophy, *Historisches Wörterbuch der Philosophie*, devotes sixty-three columns of close print to the meaning of the one German word *Dialektik*. The word *Aufklärung* is somewhat simpler—it receives only sixteen columns. There is thus a tremendous amount that could be said about the combination "dialectic of enlightenment," and we shall have to limit what we say.

The word "dialectic" is related to "dialog." A dialectic is first and foremost a movement of dialog, i.e. the movement that is kept going in an open discussion between two participants with contrary opinions. It is a movement of thinking that travels through oppositions and that evidently has to serve to bring the participants together and to clarify the issues. Such a dialectic tends towards clarification and enlightenment. When Habermas argues for dialog that is free from domination ("herrschaftsfreie Dialog"), it is this original sense of dialectic and dialog that is clearly audible. Of course there is the sad possibility, which Habermas himself recognizes, that the door gets slammed and that viewpoints harden and polarize. In that case dialectic is not a path *towards* enlightenment but a dialectic *of* enlightenment. It leads from enlightenment back to its opposite, the eye that is evil, the light that is darkness.

Dialectic, as a development via oppositions, is not strictly tied to the medium of language, discussion, or thought. "Dialectic" can also signify a social trend or movement, a social evolution via oppositions. Conflict, for instance, may be the very means of reconciling people. Or growing oppression may be the very thing that launches revolution and liberation. Here too, however, on the social level, things can start to move backwards, and the progression that humans hope for can reverse into regression. Revolution certainly does not always lead to liberation. Pierre Vergniaud, the great orator of the Girondists during the French revolution, has often been quoted for his remark that revolution devours its own children. We do not have to cast doubt on the freedom-loving intentions of men like Marat, Saint-Just, and Robespierre in the French

Reign of Terror, or Trotsky and Lenin in the Russian Revolution, in order to see the dictatorship that resulted from their efforts. Here again the dialectic *towards* enlightenment ended up as a dialectic *of* enlightenment. Why? As the Dutch Christian statesman Groen van Prinsterer once said: "Revolution went further than was intended because it was not the will of men that triumphed but the power of principles."[2]

This brings us to a third and extremely problematic meaning of dialectic, a philosophical view that sees culture and history, and even world history as a whole, constructed according to principles that develop or unfold via oppositions. Here we also meet the Neo-Marxist view in which human civilization stands marked by a central dialectical motive, the principle of rational enlightenment, the principle that aimed at human dignity and liberation but brought subservience and domination. Originally at the mercy of cosmic forces and natural instincts, humans freed themselves from this tyranny by rational insight. They learned to subdue nature around them and nature inside them, to make provision for their material needs, and thus to delineate themselves as free beings. But again this cultural and historical dialectic was harboring a demon. Particularly in modern times, reason has gone into reverse. Enlightenment has made an about-turn into blindness. It could no longer keep the urge to dominate under control. The "principle of domination," formerly embodied in the outside world of nature, has now implanted itself in the inside world or "second nature" of our selves as well. It has crept into the whole of culture and society, and so it tyrannizes humankind.

Once again, this perspective is a philosophical construction of history. Certainly as a model or mold into which all of human history is to be fitted, it invites serious objections (4.3). Insofar as humans can understand these things—and our knowledge is fragmentary here—the history of civilization is not universally characterized by an urge to increasingly dominate nature. On the contrary, the early development of the natural sciences shows that empirical and experimental insights were greeted with suspicion and contempt by all sorts of groups and cultures. Such things were tolerated, as Habermas quite rightly remarked, only in subsystems of human society (6.2). It is only as an analysis of the mod-

---

2. "De revolutie is verder gegaan dan men bedoelde, omdat niet de wil der mensen, [maar] de kracht der beginselen heeft getriumfeerd" (Groen van Prinsterer, *Ongeloof en Revolutie*, 203f., 210).

ern period and of recent cultural development that the characterization hits the mark. And even then only to a limited extent.

It was during the Enlightenment of the eighteenth century that "modern" individuals, relying on enlightened reason, did indeed want to free themselves from all external ties and alien powers, including divine authority. This motive of maturity in terms of autonomous and secular freedom drove people along, subduing the world and rationalizing society without any reservations or restraint, until they themselves turned out to be victims of their own efforts, and the contemporary cultural crisis revealed itself. There are many different analyses of culture that give a place to this tension between freedom and domination. But it is the Neo-Marxists' merit that they have persistently indicated that the source of this tension is the antagonism of two principles, the motive of freedom and the motive of domination, as hidden in the notion of enlightenment reason from the very start.[3]

I admire this criticism by the Frankfurt scholars. It is an incisive critique that not only exposes communism and capitalism as affiliated models of organizing modern society but also gets down to the fundamental roots of our present distress, namely the ideas of the eighteenth century enlightenment. And they have achieved this in full knowledge that they are themselves heirs of the enlightenment. It is an exceptional example of social criticism that is simultaneously self-criticism. However, it remains to be seen whether this self-criticism is adequate.

At this point I want to stress that I share the Neo-Marxist view of the incisive significance of the enlightenment for our day. But I have my reservations concerning the question of whether the *whole* of modern cultural life can be logically or philosophically reduced to this historical starting point. If one portrays an entire period of history or even history as a whole as an immanent unfolding and drawn-out antagonism of the enlightenment, isn't the portrayal itself also totalitarian? I consider this sort of dialectic to be an unwarranted extrapolation of historical tendencies. It results in philosophical speculation, that's to say, in a metaphysical construction of world history. For the claim that the dialectic of enlightenment can be seen as an "immanent logic of history" from its

---

3. Cf. Dooyeweerd, *New Critique*, vol.1, 62–63, 197–98, 354–56. Dooyeweerd calls this antagonistic source "the religious ground-motive of Humanism", p. 190.

very beginning has no substance to it. Like all metaphysics, it cannot be refuted but neither can it be proved.[4]

Dialectic as Belief and Myth (3)

I regard all the mega-constructions that dialectical thinkers put upon the universal history of humankind as speculative. What is not speculative but thoroughly concrete is a *belief* in such mega-constructions. The belief in the dialectic of history has been a reality since Hegel and Marx, and, indeed, a reality that has rocked the world. This brings us to a fourth and final sense of the word "dialectic"—dialectic as an expression of belief.

Dialectics can be the expression of a belief in the sense of a basic commitment to an ultimate truth. It often appears in that quality nowadays. This basic belief may assume the name of class struggle, self-emancipation, cultural revolution, "the long march through the institutions" (Antonio Gramsci), "conscientization" or whatever. Through all of this, it is a belief in the latent forces and inherent potential of history. As belief it is indeed capable of quickening the pulses of millions by *touching* their hearts. My point is that a dialectic, in the sense of a submerged faith commitment, also turns up in the thoughts of the Frankfurt scholars. Here it goes under the name of "dialectic of enlightenment" and it is capable of *breaking* human hearts.

It is hard to understand why "critical theorists" who have rallied round the flag of *Aufklärung* have not clarified the ultimate presuppositions of their belief. Yet their own words speak volumes. Right at the beginning of *Dialectic of Enlightenment* Horkheimer and Adorno claim that "freedom in society is inseparable from enlightenment thinking." And they do so on the basis of what they themselves call their *petitio principii*, their starting-point without rational justification, their axiomatic belief in the liberating power of enlightenment (2.0). Their critical theory may well put on a good Marxist front as a scientific theory "that urges a transformation of society as a whole." But what drives them along

---

4. I do not believe that the Reformation, for instance, belongs to the *Aufklärung* movement; nor, for that matter, do Catholic movements of renewal. Yet the Reformation and other traditions are indispensable factors in Western history. Unlike the *Aufklärung*, the Reformation acknowledges a Lord and not the "lordship" of domination, and it sees itself in a messianic light, not in the ideological dazzle of the light of reason. See further 9.4 below.

deep down is not theoretical reason itself but their belief in the interrelation of theory and praxis—their belief that the theory both should and can expose the immanent antagonism of social contradictions in daily life and thus unleash the dialectic of liberation. It is a belief that comes under attack but one that they nevertheless cling to, however remote theory may seem from practice (2.3).

We saw how Marcuse also jumps straight in with the "dialectic of civilization," the dialectic that aims at freedom and puts on the pressure. Marcuse wrestles with Freud's work, trying not to see this dialectic as a necessary consequence of nature, an inevitable doom (3.4). The good thing about Marcuse is that his criticism, especially in *One Dimensional Man*, penetrates to the ineradicable personal responsibility of humans themselves, for, despite all dialectic, human beings "project" their world and their culture in pre-rational freedom (4.2). At the same time we had to note that Marcuse later on subordinates this subjective act of choice again to the objective necessity of historical dialectical development. He puts the act of choice in this objective setting and speaks of "the ingression of liberty into historical necessity" (4.4).

Nonetheless Marcuse continues to come up with some surprising comments. At a conference of British "anti-psychiatrists" in London in 1967 Marcuse managed to contribute a fruitful remark, despite the accusations of black activist Stokely Carmichael that the white participants were indulging in "intellectual masturbation" with their left-wing theories. He remarked: "We are dealing with the dialectics of liberation (actually a redundant phrase, because I believe that all dialectic is liberation) . . . . It is liberation from the repressive, from a bad, a false system . . ., liberation by forces developing within such a system. That is a decisive point. And liberation by virtue of the contradiction generated by the system, precisely because it is a bad, a false system."[5] A striking quotation, in which the author casually refers to a belief (note the "I believe" in the first sentence) that clutches at the dialectic of history, however negative it may appear.

A further point can be added here. Confronted by the self-consolidation of modern capitalism and by the frightening "halt in the dialectic of negativity," Marcuse was on one occasion brave enough to raise a problematic question about the dialectic of history as professed by both Hegel and Marx. He spoke of the "questionable" idea that negation could

---

5. See Cooper (ed.), *Dialectics of Liberation*, 175.

"unfold as liberation *within* an existing whole." He then emphasized the need "to reconnect the interior to the exterior on which it is dependent in history." A profound thought. Yet in my opinion Marcuse's theoretical vision of the repressive totality does not leave room for such a view, i.e. for a liberation from outside (whatever that may be taken to mean for him).[6]

It is only when one perceives Marcuse's basic belief that one can understand the deepest motivation of his theory. So far as theory is concerned in itself, he remains trapped in a strange vicious circle, because, as he says himself, revolution presupposes freedom and freedom presupposes revolution (4.4). The same vicious circle surrounds Adorno's theory in *Negative Dialectics*. For the criticism that Adorno is looking for (even if it is meant to be no more than the voice of suffering) presupposes uncorrupted thinking, while uncorrupted thinking presupposes criticism (5.2).

Adorno is so gripped by the dialectic of history and its negative apotheosis, total mythological blindness (the *totum* is totem), that he wants to find a theoretical escape from the vicious circle by postulating an "irrational catastrophe," a metaphysical fall into sin by prehistoric man. Original sin is evidently intended to lend plausibility to the remnants of human freedom, criticism, and "yearning" (5.4). A matter of faith again!

Habermas's approach is far more finely drawn. But he too believes in the dialectic of history. His dialectic is less totalitarian, yet it is still all-embracing. Just as "labor," socially speaking, is encompassed by "interaction" (6.2), so the linear development of production is in his view encompassed by the dialectical development of praxis, the moral dialectic (7.2). And Habermas also reaches the frightening conclusion that this dialectic has been brought to a halt, paralyzed amid power and ideological violence (7.5). Doesn't this mean that the therapeutic effect of "communication without domination" is left up in the air? What will mend the short-circuit in communication? In my view, the sole justification for Habermas's idea of communication is his faith in the dialectic of morality, a dialectic from which, even in the ideological blindness of today, he expects salvation (7.4).

---

6. Marcuse spoke of "die Fragwürdigkeit des Begriffs der sich *im Innern* eines bestehenden Ganzes als Befreiung entfaltenden Negation" and of the need "das Innerhalb wieder mit dem Außerhalb zu verbinden, auf das es in der Geschichte angewiesen ist" ("Zum Begriff," 185, 188, 190; see 4.4 above).

In his later years Horkheimer no longer yielded to such an irrational belief, and we ought to respect him for this intellectual integrity. The dialectic of the enlightenment gives no reason to hope for a second enlightenment. Horkheimer therefore wants to restrict himself to the bitter observation that society is marching towards an automated world. But does Horkheimer really restrict himself to this observation? I don't think so. For him too there is more at stake, a religious belief, or perhaps better a religious unbelief, that determines the real character of his vision of the future. For the observation of an actual trend is not enough to justify talk of "the immanent logic of history" (8.1) and it is not sufficient reason to resign oneself to the "administered world." Horkheimer has said "According to its meaning the way to complete administration has been laid down in history."[7] It seems no more than a statement, but I'm afraid that anyone that believes it will make it into a self-fulfilling prophecy. The *dogma* of the dialectic creates accomplices (8.4).[8]

We have seen that the word 'dialectics' has many meanings. There is no reason to reject the notion of dialectic in itself. But we are forced to conclude that within the Hegelian and Marxist tradition the word has grown into a hidden faith regarding the inevitable course of history. History is characterized as developing via oppositions and at this moment necessarily leading to an ominous reversal of reason.

Some readers may perhaps feel that this is the point at which to break off the discussion with these "dogmatic Marxists." But, for one thing, there is the question of whether a philosophical discussion ought ever to reach that point. And, apart from that, we should ask whether the desire to cut the discussion off does not equally betray a dogmatic prejudice, a belief in the so-called self-sufficiency of reason and in the closed logical nature of scientific debate. Leszek Kolakowski, a Polish Neo-Marxist who was expelled from the Party and now lives in Britain, has disputed this self-sufficient status of reason. He once remarked that scientific reason is constantly turning into a myth within Marxism, the myth of "immaculate reason" and "scientific ideology."[9] This is indeed

---

7. In *Verwaltete Welt?* 35.

8. In an interview published in the Free University's magazine, Rohrmoser quite rightly maintains that the nihilism which the critical theorists are trying to ward off has in fact got through their defenses. See Klapwijk and Griffioen, "Kritiek op de kritische theorie."

9. Kolakowski, *Mensch ohne Alternative*, 31.

a glimmer of new light within Marxist circles. The only question is whether philosophy outside Marxist circles is also willing to criticize this pretended self-sufficiency.

Thus I do not think the Frankfurt School philosophers should be reproached for the fact that their critical theory depends on an attitude of faith and ultimate commitment. The reproach is that their theory has not been sufficiently critical to acknowledge this pre-theoretical starting point. Thus theoretical reason pretends to be a force all on its own, and faith in the dialectic becomes a self-evident dogma, although it is ignored. And in fact, strange though it may sound, this hidden dogma begins to show mythical traits, just like Kolakowski noticed. For if myth, in the original sense of the word, is a belief in the mysterious forces of nature that are imbued with an immanent spirit, where does that leave the modern belief in the hidden advance towards an automated world driven along by "the immanent logic of history"?

The Messianic Light (4)

Is it really true that the Frankfurt School theorists, with their criticism of the resurrected myths and ideologies of modern times, have failed to notice the blinding myth of the dialectic, the spell under which they themselves have been working? Adorno did actually refer to this in one of the most moving passages in his *Minima Moralia*. He says there that he finds himself and this world spellbound. He denounces, of all things, the light of critical reason. In his despair he cries out for a standpoint based on redemption. He searches for a light—he calls it a "messianic light"—that will shine out of the position of redemption upon the world: "The only philosophy which can be responsibly practised in face of despair is the attempt to contemplate all things as they would present themselves from the standpoint of redemption. Knowledge has no light but that shed on the world by redemption: all else is reconstruction, mere technique. Perspectives must be fashioned that will displace and estrange the world, reveal it to be, with its rifts and crevices, as indigent and distorted as it will appear one day in the messianic light."

Adorno then adds these astonishing words: "It is the simplest of all things, because the situation calls imperatively for such knowledge . . . . But it is also the utterly impossible thing because it presupposes a standpoint removed, even though by a hair's breadth, from the scope of existence."[10] It is as if Adorno steps forward to illustrate John's Gospel: "The light shines in the darkness and the darkness did not comprehend it."[11] The blinds are drawn down. And Adorno says that the question whether redemption is real or not makes near enough no difference, since redemption is in any case an impossible thought. In other words, the myth shines on and intercepts all other light.

Again, I agree with the Neo-Marxists that a radical theory is necessary. But what does "radical" mean? Marx once said "To be radical is to grasp things by the root. But for man the root is man himself."[12] And when man engages in radical self-criticism, he finally reveals himself in the structure of his faith, in what Ernst Bloch once called the "exterritorial" in man.[13] Whatever Bloch may have meant by this word—and it seems as though he too was unable to shake off mythology[14]—what it literally says is that human beings have to seek *the ground* (of their being) *outside themselves.*

It is at this fundamental level, I suggest, that every human being is obliged to face a choice—one that impinges prior to any philosophical reflection[15]—namely the unavoidable need to choose between what I would like to call a mythical faith and a personal faith. Admittedly, I am presenting this alternative somewhat abruptly here, for the sake of brevity. It is certainly true, however, that belief in the dialectic of history turns out to be a thoroughly mythical faith. For although this faith never entirely rids itself of the "exterritorial" element, it tries to find this external ground not in a personal relationship but in an "inner" logic of history that has been objectified and in a power of critical reason that has been made self-sufficient.

---

10. Adorno, *Minima Moralia*, §153.

11. John 1:5. Translators' Note: The Dutch has, like the original Greek, a word meaning "to grasp," which stands midway between the more intellectual sense of "comprehend" (King James Version) and the more active sense of "overcome" (Revised Standard Version).

12. "Towards the Critique," 257.

13. Bloch, *Atheismus*, §53.

14. For details, see Moltmann, *Theology of Hope*, 335ff.

15. I do hold, however, that this pre-rational (not irrational) choice of faith can be sought out through a theoretical philosophy which does not close itself off, in dogmatic or skeptical self-sufficiency, from critical reflection on the presuppositions of its own standpoint. See Klapwijk, "Science and social responsibility. Cf. Dooyeweerd, *New Critique*, vol.1, 1-99.

The Marxist faith in the dialectic of history is a faith that can move mountains—a faith that *has* moved mountains. We should not forget those that have found solace in this faith. But this faith has also shown that when it is not supported and substantiated by actual developments, it is capable of the worst. We should not forget the millions that were its victims. Mythical faith can suddenly be transformed into distrust or despair. This study of a number of Neo-Marxists has provided evidence of that. Such faith can also harden into fanaticism, as was demonstrated, for example, in Germany by the revolutionary terrorists of the Baader-Meinhoff group.

Against mythical faith I set personal faith. This is the faith that fearfully but confidently rests in what Adorno spoke of, the messianic light that comes to meet humans in judgment and redemption. I say "fearfully," because the gospel of the Messiah is a critical judgment upon all earthly righteousness and iniquity, judgment also upon the myth of the dialectic.

The gospel exposes this myth as yet another of the individual's or society's blind attempts at self-redemption. Alfred Schmidt, who edited Horkheimer's *Kritische Theorie*, wrote that it was precisely from a materialist point of view that one ought not to make a fetish of the dialectic.[16] But the dialectic of history is *by nature* a fetish, what the Bible calls an idol.

There is reason to be fearful. There is also reason to be confident. For the most basic thrust of the gospel is salvation. Cutting across the mythical belief in the inherent forces of the cosmos and the immanent potential of man is the redemptive call to faith in other forces—the regenerative forces of the age to come, the ultimate remedy of a God who remains faithful to his creation. This belief is not mythology. For it is secured and guaranteed in a personal bond with Jesus, the Messiah himself, who anticipated the future in his death and resurrection and who lets his followers partake in this precious secret. Day by day his followers stand in the messianic light, stumbling, getting to their feet again, fearful, confident, living with the rebuke of "enlightened" thinkers that they are naive and immature.[17] They *know* that man is "exterritorial" and they

---

16. In the editor's postscript to the German edition of Horkheimer's *Kritische Theorie* (vol.2, 350).

17. It is remarkable that Horkheimer arrived at a connection between critical thinking and religious faith. But one thing should be borne in mind. His "yearning for the totally other" is not exterritorial. It does not seem to be open to messianic light. It is a subjective longing for the absolute opposite of what the dialectic of history has in store

are not ashamed to know it. As long as they carry this secret with them in their lives, they remain faithful to the earth and sensitive to suffering, and, in the midst of bruised and damaged life, they renew and sharpen their critical vision. But they are shielded from presumptuousness and despondency.

---

for us. His *Sehnsucht* is nostalgia, or rather wistfulness and melancholy. In a radio interview in Berne (published as *Verwaltete Welt?*), Horkheimer later declared that religion, however indispensable, could not nowadays be anything more than sadness and sorrow. It is "the sorrow that the righteousness of which religion and theology have been telling us right up to this day, is in the final analysis nonexistent" ("die Trauer darüber, daß es jene Gerechtigkeit, von der die Religion, die Theologie gesprochen hat and auch heute noch spricht, in letzter Linie nicht gibt," *Verwaltete Welt?* 35).

Bibliography

Adorno, T. W. *Ästhetische Theorie,* In *Gesammelte Schriften,* vol.7. Edited by G. Adorno and R. Tiedemann. Frankfurt: Suhrkamp Verlag, 1973.
———. *Minima Moralia: Reflections from Damaged Life.* Translated by E. F. N. Jephcott. London: NLB, 1974.
———. *Minima Moralia: Reflexionen aus dem beschädigten Leben.* In *Gesammelte Schriften,* vol.4. 1970.
———. *Negative Dialectics.* Translated by E.B. Ashton. New York: Seabury, 1973.
———. *Negative Dialektik.* 2nd ed. In *Gesammelte Schriften,* vol.6. 1970.
Adorno, T. W., and M. Horkheimer. *Dialectic of Enlightenment,* see Horkheimer, M. and T. W. Adorno.
———. *Dialektik der Aufklärung,* see Horkheimer, M. and T.W. Adorno.
Adorno, T.W., et al. *Der Positivismusstreit in der deutschen Soziologie.* Neuwied/Berlin: Hermann Luchterhand, 1971.
———. *The Positivist Dispute in German Sociology.* Translated by G. Adey and D. Frisby. London: Heinemann, 1972.
Bekker, B. *De Betoverde Weereld.* Amsterdam: Daniel van den Dalen, 1692.
Benjamin W. "Lehre vom Ähnlichen." In *Zur Aktualität Walter Benjamins,* edited by Siegfried Unseld, 23ff. Frankfurt: Suhrkamp, 1973.
Bloch, E. *Atheismus im Christentum.* Frankfurt: Suhrkamp, 1968.
———. *Philosophische Grundfragen,* vol.1. Frankfurt: Suhrkamp, 1961.
———. *Das Prinzip Hoffnung.* Frankfurt: Suhrkamp, 1959.
Dooyeweerd, H. *A New Critique of Theoretical Thought.* Translated by D.H. Freeman and W.S. Young. 4 vols. Lewiston, NY: Edwin Mellen, 1997.
———. *In the Twilight of Western Thought: Studies in the Pretended Autonomy of Philosophical Thought* (1960), edited by K.A. Smith. Lewiston, NY: Edwin Mellen, 1999.
———. *Roots of Western Culture: Pagan, Secular, and Christian Options* (1945-48). Translated by J. Kraay and edited by M. Vander Vennen and B. Zylstra, newly edited by D. F. M. Strauss. Lewiston, NY: Edwin Mellen, 2003.
Freud, S. "Beyond the Pleasure Principle." In *Standard Edition,* vol.18, 7-64.
———. "Civilization and Its Discontents." In *Standard Edition,* vol.14, 59-243.
———. *General Introduction to Psychoanalysis,* New York: Garden City, 1943.
———. "Introductory Lectures on Psychoanalysis." In *Standard Edition,* vol.15, part 1, 3-79; part 2, 83-238; and vol.16, part 3, 239-463.
———. "Jenseits des Lustprinzips." In *Gesammelte Werke,* vol.13. Frankfurt: Fisher, 1967.
———. *The Standard Edition of the Complete Psychological* Works *of Sigmund Freud.* Translated and edited by J. Strachey in collaboration with Anna Freud. London: Hogarth, 1961.

Bibliography

———. "Das Unbehagen in der Kultur." In *Gesammelte Schriften*, vol.14.

———. *Vorlesungen zur Einführung in die Psychoanalyse*, Leipzig/Zurich/Wien: Internationaler Psychoanalytischer Verlag, 1926.

Freud in der Gegenwart: Ein Vortragszyklus der Universitäten Frankfurt und Heidelberg zum hundertsten Geburtstag, Frankfurter Beiträge zur Soziologie, vol.6. Frankfurt: Europäische Verlagsanstalt, 1957.

Fromm, E. "Die gesellschaftliche Bedingtheit der psychoanalytischen Therapie," *Zeitschrift für Sozialforschung* 4 (1935), 365–97.

Garaudy, R., et al. *L'homme chrétien et l'homme marxiste*. Paris/Geneva: La Palatine, 1964.

Groen van Prinsterer, G. *Ongeloof en revolutie: Een reeks van historische voorlezingen*. Kampen: J. H. Kok, 1922.

Habermas, J. "The Analytical Theory of Science and Dialectics" and "A Positivistically Bisected Rationalism." In Adorno et al., *The Positivist Dispute*, 131–62, 198–225.

———. "Analytische Wissenschaftstheorie und Dialektik." In Adorno et al., *Der Positivismusstreit*, 155–91.

———. "Bewußtmachende oder rettende Kritik – die Aktualität Walter Benjamins." In *Zur Aktualität Walter Benjamins*,189 ff. Frankfurt: Suhrkamp, 1973.

———. *Erkenntnis und Interesse*. 2nd ed. Frankfurt: Suhrkamp, 1973.

———. "Zum Geleit," In *Antworten auf Herbert Marcuse*, 9–16. Frankfurt: Suhrkamp, 1968.

———. *Knowledge and Human Interests*. Translated by J.J. Shapiro. Boston: Beacon, 1971.

———. "A Postscript to *Knowledge and Human Interests*." In *Philosophy of the Social Sciences*, vol.3, 157–89 (1973).

———. "Ein philosophierender Intellektueller." In *Über Theodor W. Adorno*, 35–43. Frankfurt: Suhrkamp, 1970.

———. *Strukturwandel der Öffentlickeit: Untersuchungen zu einer Kategorie der bürgerlichen Gesellschaft*. Neuwied/Berlin: Hermann Luchterhand, 1962.

———. *Technik und Wissenschaft als "Ideologie."* 5th ed. Frankfurt: Suhrkamp, 1971.

———. *Theorie und Praxis: Sozialphilosophische Studien*. 4th ed. Frankfurt: Suhrkamp, 1971.

———. *Theory and Practice*. Translated by J. Viertel. London: Heinemann, 1974.

———. *The Theory of Communicative Action* (1981). Translated by Thomas McCarthy, vol.1: *Reason and the Rationalization of Society*; vol.2: *Lifeworld and System: A Critique of Functionalist Reason*. Boston: Beacon, 1984, 1987.

———. *Towards a Rational Society: Student Protest, Science, and Politics*. Translated by J. J. Shapiro. Boston: Beacon, 1970.

Harmsen, G. *Natuur, geschiedenis, filosofie*. Nijmegen: SUN, 1975.

Hegel, G. W. F. *Phänomenologie des Geistes, Sämtlichte Werke*, vol.5, Hamburg: Felix Meiner, 1952.

———. *Phenomenology of Mind*. Translated by J. B. Baille. Atlantic Highlands, NJ: Humanities, 1964.

Hoeven, J. van der, et al. *Marxisme en Revolutie*. Amsterdam: Buijten & Schipperheijn, 1967.

Horkheimer, M. *Anfänge der bürgerlichen Geschichtsphilosophie*. Stuttgart: Kohlhammer, 1930.

———. *Critical Theory: Selected Essays*. Translated by M.J. O'Connell et al. New York: Herder and Herder, 1972.
———. *Critique of Instrumental Reason*. Translated by M.J. O'Connell et al. New York: Seabury, 1974.
———. *Eclipse of Reason*. Translated by M.J. O'Connell et al. Oxford: Oxford University Press/New York: Seabury, 1974.
———. *Zur Kritik der instrumentellen Vernuft: Aus den Vorträgen und Aufzeichnungen seit Kriegsende*, edited by A. Schmidt. 2nd ed. Frankfurt: Fischer, 1974.
———. *Kritische Theorie: Eine Dokumentation*, 2 vols. Frankfurt: Fischer, 1968.
———. *Die Sehnsucht nach dem ganz Anderen: Ein Interview mit Kommentar*, edited by H. Gumnior. Hamburg: Furche, 1970.
———. *Verwaltete Welt? Ein Gespräch*. Zurich: Die Arche, 1970.
Horkheimer, M., and T.W. Adorno. *Dialectic of Enlightenment: Philosophical Fragments* (1947). Translated by E. Jephcott and edited by G. Schmid Noerr. Stanford, CA: Stanford University Press, 2002.
———. *Dialektik der Aufklärung: Philosophische Fragmente*. 2nd ed. Frankfurt: Fischer, 1969.
Houten, B. C. van. *Tussen aanpassing en kritiek: De derde methodenstrijd in de Duitse sociologie*. Deventer: Van Loghum Slaterus, 1970.
Jay, M. *The Dialectical Imagination: A History of the Frankfurt School and the Institute for Social Research 1923–1950*. Boston: Little Brown and Company, 1973.
Klapwijk, J. "Antithesis, Synthesis, and the Idea of Transformational Philosophy." *Philosophia Reformata* 51 (1986), 138–52. [http://jacobklapwijk.nl/].
———. *Dialektiek der verlichting: Een verkenning in het neomarxisme van de Frankfurter Schule*. Assen: Van Gorcum, 1976, 2nd ed. 1977.
———. "Geloof en rede in de theologie van Troeltsch en Pannenberg." In Klapwijk et al. (eds.), *Vrede met de rede?* 63–83.
———. "Reformational Philosophy on the Boundary between the Past and the Future." *Philosophia Reformata* 52 (1987), 101–34. [http://jacobklapwijk.nl/]
———. "Science and Social Responsibility in Neo-Marxist and Christian Perspective," in: P. Blokhuis et al. (eds.), *Wetenschap, wijsheid, filosoferen: Opstellen aangeboden aan Hendrik van Riessen* (Assen: Van Gorcum, 1981), pp. 75-98. [http://jacobklapwijk.nl/].
———. *Tussen historisme en relativisme: Een studie over de dynamiek van het historisme en de wijsgerige ontwikkelingsgang van Ernst Troeltsch*. Assen: Van Gorcum, 1970. [http://jacobklapwijk.nl/]
Klapwijk, J., and S. Griffioen. "Kritiek op de kritische theorie," an interview with G. Rohrmoser, *VU-Magazine* 3, 8 (September 8, 1974).
Klapwijk, J., S. Griffioen, et al (eds.), *Vrede met de rede? Over het vraagstuk van rede en religie, van autonomie en heil*. Assen: Van Gorcum, 1970.
Kolakowski, L., *Marxism and Beyond: On Historical Understanding and Individual Responsibility*. Translated by Jane Zielonko Peel. London: Paladin, 1971.
———. *Der Mensch ohne Alternative: Von der Möglichkeit und Unmöglichkeit Marxist zu sein*. Munich: R. Piper, 1964.
Leeuw, J. de. *Marxisme in de culturele anthropologie*. Assen: Van Gorcum, 1976.
Lenin, V. I. *Materialism and Empirico-Criticism: Critical Comments on a Reactionary Philosophy*. Moscow: Foreign Languages, 1947.
Machovec, M. *Vom Sinn des menschlichen Lebens*. Freiburg: Rombach, 1971.

Marcuse, H. "Zum Begriff der Negation in der Dialektik." In *Ideen zu einer kritischen Theorie der* Gesellschaft, 185–90. Frankfurt: Suhrkamp, 1969.

———. *Eros and Civilization: A Philosophical Inquiry into Freud.* 2nd ed. Boston: Beacon, 1966.

———. "Freedom and Freud's Theory of Instincts" and "The Obsolescence of the Freudian Concept of Man." In *Five lectures: Psychoanalysis, Politics and Utopia.* Translated by J. J. Shapiro and S. M. Weber, 1–27, 44–61. Boston: Allen Lane, 1970.

———. "Industrialisierung und Kapitalismus im Werke Max Webers" and "Das Veralten der Psychoanalyse." In: *Kultur und Gesellschaft,* vol. 2, 85–129. Frankfurt: Suhrkamp, 1968.

———. "Industrialisation and Capitalism in the Work of Max Weber." In *Negations: Essays in Critical Theory.* Ttranslated by J. J. Shapiro, 68ff. London: Allen Lane, 1968.

———. "Liberation from the Affluent Society." In D. Cooper, editor, *The Dialectics of Liberation,* 175–92. Harmondsworth: Penguin, 1971.

———. *One-Dimensional Man: Studies in the Ideology of Advanced Industrial Society.* London: Routledge & Kegan Paul, 1964.

———. *Reason and Revolution: Hegel and the Rise of Social Theory.* London: Routledge & Kegan Paul, 1973.

———. "Trieblehre und Freiheit." In *Freud in der Gegenwart,* 425–41.

Marx, K. *Capital I,* edited by F. Engels. Translated by S. Moore and E. Aveling. Moscow: Progress, 1954.

———. *Critique of Hegel's "Philosophy of Right."* Translated by A. Jolin and J. O'Malley and edited by J. O'Malley. Cambridge: Cambridge University Press, 1970.

———. "Die deutsche Ideologie." In *Die Frühschriften,* edited by S. Landshut, 341–417. Stuttgart: Alfred Kröner, 1968.

———. "Economic and Philosophic Manuscripts of 1844." In K. Marx and F. Engels, *Collected Works,* vol. 3.

———. "The German Ideology." In ibid, vol.5, 341–485.

———. *Das Kapital: Zur Kritik der politischen Ökonomie.* Berlin: Dietz, 1975.

———. "Zur Kritik der Hegelschen Rechtsphilosophie." In *Die Frühschriften,* 207–24.

———. "Nationalökonomie und Philosophie." In ibid., 225–316.

———. "Thesen über Feuerbach." In ibid., 339–41.

———. "Theses on Feuerbach." In *Writings of the Young Marx on Philosophy and Society,* edited by L. D. Easton and K. H. Guddat, 400–2. New York: Doubleday, 1967.

———. "Towards the Critique of Hegel's Philosophy of Law." In ibid., 246–64.

Marx K. and F. Engels. *Collected Works.* London: Lawrence and Wisehart, 1976.

Moltmann, J. *Theologie der Hoffnung: Untersuchungen zur Begründung und zu den Konsequenzen einer christlichen Eschatologie.* Serie Beiträge zur evangelischen Theologie 38. Munich: Chr. Kaiser, 1964.

———. *Theology of Hope: On the Ground and Implications of a Christian Eschatology.* Translated by J.W. Leitch. London, SCM, 1969.

O'Rourke, J. J. *The Problem of Freedom in Marxist Thought: An Analysis of the Treatment of Human Freedom by Marx, Engels, Lenin, and Contemporary Soviet Philosophy.* Dordrecht/Boston: D. Reidel, 1974.

Rohrmoser, G. "Autonomie." In *Handbuch philosophischer Grundbegriffe,* vol.1, 155–70. Munich: Kösel, 1973.

———. *Das Elend der kritischen Theorie: Theodor W. Adorno, Herbert Marcuse, Jürgen Habermas.* Freiburg: Rombach, 1973.

———. "De problematiek van de rede in het perspektief van het neomarxisme van de Frankfurter Schule." In Klapwijk et al., *Vrede met de rede?* 87–96.

Schmidt, A. "Existential-Ontologie und historische Materialismus bei Herbert Marcuse." In *Antworten auf Herbert Marcuse*, 17ff. Frankfurt: Suhrkamp, 1968.

———. "Nachwort des Herausgebers." In Horkheimer, *Kritische Theorie*, 333–59.

Schuurman, E. *Technology and the Future: A Philosophical Challenge*. Translated by H. D. Morton. Grand Rapids: The Reformational Publishing Project and Paideia, 2009.

Steenbergen, B. van. "Jürgen Habermas." In *Filosofie van de 20e Eeuw*, edited by C. P. Bertels and E. Petersma, 175–90. Assen: Van Gorcum, 1972.

Theunissen, M. *Gesellschaft und Geschichte: Zur Kritik der kritischen Theorie*. Berlin: Walter de Gruyter, 1969.

Vollenhoven, D. H. Th. *A Vollenhoven Reader*. Translated and edited by J. H. Kok. Sioux Center, IA: Dordt College, 2010 (forthcoming).

Zuidema, S. U. *De revolutionaire maatschappijkritiek van Herbert Marcuse*. Amsterdam: Buijten & Schipperheijn, 1970.

Zuidervaart L. *Adorno's Aesthetic Theory: The Redemption of Illusion*. Cambridge, MA: MIT, 1991.

———. *Refractions: Truth in Adorno's Aesthetic Theory*. Toronto: University of Toronto, 1981.

———. *Social Philosophy after Adorno*. Cambridge: Cambridge University Press, 2007.

Subject/Name Index

A

absolute, 12, 41, 45, 47, 51–53, 65–67, 72–73, 76, 80–81, 97
Adorno, Theodor W., vii–viii, x–xii, 1–7, 9–18, 20–23, 28, 31, 34–35, 42, 43–53, 54–56, 63, 66, 77, 79–81, 86, 88, 91–97
alienation, 5, 18, 30, 50, 69
America, viii, 10, 15, 19, 34, 82
Apel, Karl-Otto, 86
Aristotle, 37
Aufklärung. *See* Enlightenment
automation, automated, 1, 5, 27, 30–31, 34, 61
  automatons, automated world, 28, 79, 84–85, 94–95
autonomy, autonomous, ix, 3, 10, 17, 47, 52, 59, 75–77, 90

B

Bacon, Francis, 16, 64
Bekker, Balthasar, 2
belief (religious), 5, 61, 91–97
Benjamin, Walter, 5, 7, 51
Bloch, Ernst, 37, 52, 81, 96

C

Campanella, Tommaso, 11
capitalism, 5–6, 59–62, 72, 87, 90, 92
Carmichael, Stokeley, 92
catastrophe, 49–50, 91
communication, communicative, xi, 57–59, 61–63, 70–77, 93
  communicative turn, ix

communism, communist, 2, 56, 61–62, 71, 79, 87
Cooper, David, 92
critical theory, vii–ix, 2–4, 14–18, 30, 40–42, 50–51, 64–65, 80, 83–86, 95
criticism, critique, ix–x, 3, 9, 12–13, 16–18, 21, 28, 34, 49–54, 65, 75, 83, 86–87, 92–95
  self-criticism, 10, 46, 90, 96
  social criticism, 20, 40, 74, 85, 90

D

death, 22, 28, 52, 83, 85–87, 97
  death-instinct, 21, 25–27, 31, 34
  Thanatos, 25–26
Descartes, René, 37
dialectic, dialectical, viii–ix, 5–7, 32, 37, 41–47, 62–64, 69–72, 75, 84, 88–91
  ethical, of morality, 69–71, 73, 77, 93
  meaning of dialectics, 2, 88–95
  negative dialectics, 7, 42–55, 57, 59, 62–66, 73, 78–79, 84–85, 88–91
  of culture, civilization, 19, 23, 26, 28, 30, 36, 92
  of enlightenment, x, 1–7, 14–19, 21, 28, 30, 36, 42–43, 46, 48–49, 53
  of history, ix, 16–17, 39, 76, 91–93, 96–97
  of liberation, 41, 77, 92
  of reason, 7, 29, 35, 39, 47, 63–64
domination, 3, 9, 34, 37–40, 44, 47–49, 62–63, 70, 77, 87–91, 93
  principle of domination, 33, 38, 87, 89
Dooyeweerd, Herman, viii–ix, 90, 96

E

eclipse of reason. *See* reason
ego, superego, 22, 28, 34–35, 85
Engels, Friedrich, 14, 51
Enlightenment, xi, 2–3, 5–6, 9–10, 12–13, 37, 82, 90
   dialectic of enlightenment. *See* dialectic
eros, 7, 26, 33–34, 38–39
erotic, erotization, 19, 25–26, 31, 85
exterritorial, ix, 96–97

F

faith, ix, 5–6, 39, 61, 76, 80–81, 91, 93–97
   mythical faith, 4, 96–97
   personal faith, ix, 96–97
fascism, 1–2, 5, 11
   left-wing fascism, 77
fatherless society, 27
fetish, fetishism, 6, 44, 54, 64, 72, 97
Feuerbach, Ludwig, 41, 67
Fichte, Johann Gottlieb, 68–69
Frankfurt School, 3, 6, 15, 19–20, 51–52, 54–55, 72–73, 86, 95
freedom, viii, xi, 2–5, 9, 17, 30–36, 39–40, 49–51, 58–59, 74, 77–80, 84–85, 88, 90–93
Freud, Sigmund, 6, 19–31, 33–36, 68, 74, 92
Fromm, Erich, 19–21

G

Galilei, Galileo, 37
ganz Andere, 51, 79, 83
Garaudy, Roger, 81
Gehlen, Arnold, 56
God, 52, 80–84, 97
Griffioen, Sander, 94
Groen van Prinsterer, Guillaume, 89
ground motive, 8, 90
Gumnior, Helmut, 83

H

Habermas, Jürgen, viii–x, 5, 7–8, 15, 19, 36, 39, 53, **54–64, 65–78**, 82, 85–89, 93
Harmsen, Ger, 71
Hegel, Georg W. F., 5, 18, 34, 37, 40, 43, 45, 47–48, 51–52, 65–73, 75–76, 83, 91–92, 94.
Heidegger, Martin, 6, 19, 35
Herrschaft, herrschaftsfrei, 4, 44, 63, 77, 88
historicist, 29, 40
Hitler, Adolf, 15
Hoeven, Johan van der, 70
Honneth, Axel, 86
hope, principle of hope, xi, 50–53, 71, 80–81, 94, 96
Horkheimer, Max, viii, x–xi, 1–8, **9–18**, 20–23, 28, 31, 34, 37, 42, 48, 51, 54–56, 63–64, 77–78, **79–85**, 86, 88, 91, 94, 97–98
Horney, Karen, 20
Houten, Bé C. van, 78
Hugo, Victor, 82
humanism, humanistic, 12, 17, 90
humility, 13

I

identification, 5, 21, 24, 27, 34, 43–44, 46
ideology, 8, 12, 54–55, 59–61, 63–65, 68, 71–73, 94
imagination, 23, 32
instinct, instinctual, 19–29, 31, 33–35, 39, 41, 80, 89
Institute for Social Research, 9, 15, 19–20
interaction, 28, 57–64, 68–69, 71, 73–74, 93
interests, 23, 38, 53, 57–58, 74–77
   knowledge-interests. *See* knowledge

J

Jay, Martin, 20–21
Jesus, 97

K

Kant, Immanuel, 5, 47, 65–66, 68–69, 76, 78, 81–82, 84
Klapwijk, Jacob, vii–x, xii, 37, 40, 56, 76, 94, 96
knowledge, 3, 11, 16, 18, 32, 35–36, 54, 57, 63–67, 72–73, 80, 89, 95
    knowledge-interests, 57–58, 74–75
    productive, reflective, 69
    self knowledge, 12, 75
Kolakowski, Leszek, 81, 94–95

L

Landauer, Karl, 20
language, 5, 10–12, 41–42, 47, 57–59, 71, 74, 88
Leeuwe, Jules de, 71
Lenin, Vladimir I., 48, 60, 89
libido, 23–24, 26–27, 29, 31
life, 3, 22–24, 33–34, 39, 50, 54, 57, 60–61, 69, 78, 80–81, 87
    life-impulse, 11, 25–26, 31
logic, logical, 10, 44–46, 56–57
    of history, 79, 84, 90, 94–96
    of domination, 37
Low, Barbara, 25

M

Machovec, Milan, 81
Marat, Jean Paul, 88
Marcuse, Herbert, viii, x, 6–7, 9, 15, **19–32, 33–42**, 46, 48, 51–56, 63, 68, 70, 74, 77, 86, 92–93
Marx, Karl, 3, 5–6, 14–17, 20, 29, 38, 41, 44–45, 48, 51, 59–62, 65–72, 75, 81–84, 91–92, 96
materialism, materialist, 6, 14, 19, 47–48, 52, 65, 67–69, 75–76, 97
maturity, 2, 47, 49, 52, 58, 75–76, 88, 90
Max Planck Institute, viii, 54, 86
meaning, 2, 4, 44, 50, 58–59, 80–81, 84, 88–89, 94, 96
Messiah, messianic, ix, xii, 86, 91, 95, 97

metaphysics, 52–53, 76, 80, 91
mimesis, mimetic, 2, 4–5, 11, 23, 34
model, viii, 34, 47, 52, 57, 63, 69, 89–90
Moltmann, Jürgen, 96
morals, morality, 61, 69–71, 73, 76, 82, 85, 93
More, Thomas, 11
myth, mythology, ix, 3–7, 18, 44, 49, 54, 64, 72–73, 79, 85–86, 91, 93–97

N

naturalism, naturalistic, 17, 26, 28, 35–36
negation, negativity, 12–13, 40, 42, 45, 51, 69–70, 92–93
    negative dialectics. *See* dialectic
    negative thinking, theory, 35, 37, 41
Neo-Marxism, Neo-Marxist, 1–2, 6, 13, 16, 42, 65, 87, 89–90, 94, 96–97
neutral, neutrality, 20, 37–39, 55–56
New Left, vii–viii
Nietzsche, Friedrich, 6
nirvana, 25

O

object, 40, 44, 52
    objectify, objectification, 18, 28, 56, 87
    objective, objectivity, 29, 35, 40, 47–48, 72–73, 76, 92, 96
    revenge of the object. *See* revenge
    subject and object, 11, 17, 66–67
one dimensional, 7, 33–37, 39–42, 92
O'Rourke, James J., 51

P

performance principle, 29–31, 33
phenomenology, 66–67, 72–73
Plato, 37
pleasure principle, 22–27, 31, 34
political, vii, ix, xi, 14–16, 19, 33–35, 38, 41, 55–60
    political economy, 16, 60
    politically neutral, 37, 39, 56

Subject/Name Index

primal horde, 21–22, 24, 27
principal of domination. *See* domination
project, viii, x, 35–40, 92
projection, 6, 21, 53, 61
psychoanalysis, 19–22, 24, 27–29, 35, 74

R

radical, radicalism, vii, ix, 10–15, 35, 45, 54, 65–66, 73, 75, 96
rationality, 10, 29–30, 36, 38–39, 55–59, 61
reality principle, 22–31, 34
reason, ix, xi–xii, 2–13, 16–18, 22–24, 35–39, 47–50, 54–56, 76–78, 80–81, 89–92
   as unreason, 78
   critical reason, 13, 16, 41, 48, 95
   dialectic of reason. See dialectic
   eclipse of reason, 10
   practical reason, 22, 63
   self-sufficient, ix, 94–96
   technical reason, 62–63
recognition, 70, 73, 75
   self-recognition, 11–12
reconciliation, 10, 12–14, 17, 31, 51, 70, 73, 76, 84
Red Army Faction, RAF, vii
Reformation, viii, 91
reformational, viii
religion, ix, 80–84, 98
Renaissance, viii, 11, 37, 86
repression, ix, xi, 20–24, 32, 35, 49, 71, 74–75
   surplus repression, 27, 29–30, 70
responsibility, 17, 36, 38–39, 47, 61, 75, 92, 96
revenge, 7, 10, 25
   revenge of the object, 54
revisionism, 20–21
Robespierre, Maximilien F.M.I. de, 88
Robinson, John A.T., 82
Rohrmoser, Günter, 2, 50, 75–77, 86, 94

S

Saint-Just, Louis A.L. de, 88
Sartre, Jean-Paul, 35
Schelling, Friedrich W.J., 48
science, 7, 10, 30, 37–39, 47, 54–61, 64, 74–75, 82, 89, 96
   critical science/thought, vii–xii, 10–14, 40–43, 65–67, 72–75, 95–98
   traditional science, 3
Schiller, Friedrich, 31, 48
Schleyer, Hanns-Martin, vii
Schmidt, Alfred, 36, 86, 97
Schopenhauer, Arthur, 6, 81, 85
Schuurman, Egbert, 56
Sehnsucht, yearning, 11, 51–53, 79, 81–85, 93, 97–98
self-recognition. *See* recognition
Steenbergen, Bart van, 64, 78
subject, subjectivity, 6, 14, 28, 41, 44–45, 49–50, 72
   subject and object, 3, 11, 17, 35, 40, 47–48, 66–69, 92
   subjectivism, 48
suffering, ix, xi, 2, 10–11, 14–16, 47–50, 69–70, 81–83, 93, 98
Sullivan, Harry Stock, 20
surplus value, 61
synthesis through labor, 69

T

Thanatos. *See* death
theology, 52, 82, 96, 98
therapy, 22, 34, 72, 74
Theunissen, Michael, 75–76
Tiedemann, Rolf, 86
Tillich, Paul, 82
transcendental, 10, 18, 58, 66–68, 74–76
transformation, transformational, viii, 15, 24, 28, 91
Trotsky, Leon, 89

U

utopia, utopian, 6, 11, 19, 31, 33, 39–40, 46, 84

V

Vergniaud, Pierre, 88
vicious circle, 40, 42, 77, 93
Vollenhoven, Dirk H.Th., viii–ix

W

Weber, Max, 2, 55
Wellmer, Albrecht, 86
Whitehead, Alfred North, 34, 41
work, 6, 22, 30–32, 50, 56–62, 68, 74

Y

Yallop, Colin, xii
Yallop-Bergsma, Ineke, xii
yearning. *See* Sehnsucht

Z

Zuidema, Sytse Ulbe, 36
Zuidervaart, Lambert, vii, x, xii

www.ingramcontent.com/pod-product-compliance
Lightning Source LLC
Chambersburg PA
CBHW070943160426
43193CB00011B/1796